SECRETS IN YOUR NAME

1ˢᵗ   p. ~~84~~ 26
2ⁿᵈ   p. 66
3ʳᵈ

UNLOCK THE MYSTERIES OF YOUR NAME AND BIRTH DATE
THROUGH THE SCIENCE OF NUMEROLOGY

SECRETS
IN YOUR NAME

NAME YOUR CHILD FOR POTENTIAL SUCCESS AND HAPPINESS

NEIL KOELMEYER AND URSULA KOLECKI

ANGUS
& ROBERTSON
PUBLISHERS

Giving a name is indeed a poetic art.
Thomas Carlyle

ANGUS & ROBERTSON PUBLISHERS

Unit 4, Eden Park, 31 Waterloo Road,
North Ryde, NSW, Australia 2113, and
16 Golden Square, London W1R 4BN,
United Kingdom

First published in Australia
by Angus & Robertson Publishers in 1988
First published in the United Kingdom
by Angus & Robertson (UK) Ltd in 1988

Copyright © Neil Koelmeyer and Ursula Kolecki, 1988

National Library of Australia
Cataloguing-in-publication data

Koelmeyer, Neil, 1927- .
   Secrets in your name.

   ISBN 0 207 15650 6.

   1. Symbolism of numbers. I. Kolecki, Ursula, 1961-
   II. Title.

133.3'35

Typeset in 10 pt Aster
Printed in Australia by The Book Printer

C•O•N•T•E•N•T•S

WHAT IS NUMEROLOGY?

It is generally accepted that the science of numbers was introduced to the Western world by Pythagoras some 2400 years ago. Pythagoras himself gained his knowledge of numbers, among many other things, from Egypt and the Near East. Although the roots of the science of numerology are lost in the dim and distant past, some researchers have found evidence that it was practised in Egypt as far back as 13,000 years ago. However, despite these seemingly fantastic dates, this science remains as alive and active today as it was before the dawn of history. Furthermore, it is not only its antiquity that gives this fascinating study its credibility, for numerology is based on principles that do not change and proves itself over and over again in practice.

What really is numerology? It is simply the study of vibration. It is commonly defined as the esoteric interpretation of numbers. Both definitions are correct, for numbers are merely symbols of creative forces or vibratory frequencies. There is a qualitative value to numbers as well as the commonly used quantitative value. In numerology we are concerned with the qualitative value which, in fact, predates the quantitative value, as mankind used numbers as symbols of creative forces well before they were used for counting. We use, and are guided by, all sorts of symbols in our daily activities. All road signs are symbols which we cannot afford to be ignorant of or ignore. The question mark is a symbol. The x x x we use in greeting cards and personal letters are symbols of love and endearment. The numbers 1 to 9 are the symbols of numerology.

We may use number and vibration as interchangeable words. But numerology is not the study of numbers as such. A number by itself means nothing. It is the vibratory quality and power, positive or negative, symbolised by a number that we weigh and consider. So, when we think of numbers we really think in terms of vibratory frequencies that compose and influence both matter and non-matter. Everything that exists is formed and sustained in a vibratory state. In other words, the very nature of the universe is vibratory. Science has proved that all life is motion — motion of universal energy. We call this motion vibration because of its wave-like nature. Every substance, colour, shape, smell and sound has its being and is determined through vibration. In addition, abstract qualities such as individual characteristics, desires, emotions and other extra-sensory conditions are vibrations.

So when we talk of vibration we also mean number, and each number is a symbol of a particular chain of qualities. Each number from 1 to 9 represents a unique combination of personality characteristics. Particular numbers from our birth date and name play a prominent role in shaping our personality and destiny. Their effectiveness will depend on their position, their frequency of occurrence and their relationship with other numbers.

The numbers also describe the potential of our personality. However, it is up to us to choose if we will exploit the talents given to us at birth, or overdevelop negative tendencies of our personality. The numbers should describe the essential aspects of our individual characters. There is then scope for us to embrace or reject, derive benefit from or abuse the aspects described. The quality of leadership, for instance, could be benevolent or dictatorial, or business acumen could lead either to greed and ruthless competition or the acquisition of wealth through sound judgement and hard work.

It is important that we understand ourselves and our motivations, and no meaningful relationship can be built without a similar appreciation of others. A study of numerology could help develop this insight. This may help us recognise the reasons behind some apparently illogical or inexplicable actions of another, or perhaps ourselves. A clear understanding of the motivations of others can be acquired, and with this knowledge comes tolerance.

Numerology informs us of our assets and shortcomings and encourages us to make the best of the former and improve and control the latter. The character analysis tells us about our general personality traits and our potential strengths and weaknesses. It suggests suitable employment and pastimes and examines how we handle financial resources. Our social habits and our reactions to various relationships are revealed. Numerology can play a considerable part in establishing a harmonious relationship in personal life as well as in business.

If we want to set up a business partnership and the numbers indicate that neither of us has a flair for business, we could be courting disaster. But if, through a numerological analysis, we are made aware of the inherent risk and get sound advice and employ a competent accountant, the lack of financial acumen or administrative talents need not be a liability. Similarly, if we are not the domesticated type we will probably only cause unhappiness to ourselves and our partner if we choose as a partner someone whose numbers indicate that he or she will insist on financial security, a large family and strict domesticity.

In all types of relationships it would be helpful to do some numerological research on the person or persons who will be involved in decisions we need to make from time to time. This exercise could give us some insight into how much our associates may need to compromise themselves to accommodate our needs and, in turn, how much we will need to concede. If the accusation "You're always making unreasonable demands" has been levelled at us, this type of inquiry could expose the need for further personality investigation. For the sake of harmony, we may then choose not to broach a subject if we know the reaction is likely to be unfavourable.

If our career is to take us to another State, for example, we can ascertain how adaptable our partner may be to this change. If we are considering lending a substantial sum of money or goods of value to someone, it will be wise to make some numerological inquiries as to whether we are likely to see our money or goods again. Philosophers argue that we will never have all the information we need at the time when we must make a decision, but still it must be made and we therefore must always take some kind of risk. Numerology can help us by providing some insight into personality, motivations and likely actions of people and thus reduce the human risk factors involved in making decisions. As many of us are not skilled judges of character and wish we had the patience and ability to develop greater psychological intuition, the principles of numerology could be summoned to our aid in every department of human activity.

Counsellors and welfare and social workers could find a

useful new perspective on how to handle their clients by the use of numerology. This science suggests that if people work towards making their positive contribution on this earth by pursuing the fulfilment of their destiny, they will be less frustrated and more satisfied with life and reap greater rewards. Awareness of the personality types of people in difficulty, and their destinies, may prove valuable to counsellors and help them steer their clients in directions where scope for development of their potential is greatest.

There may be conflict between the personality type, the directions of destiny and natural talents of an individual. The personality may be dominant and antagonistic towards adapting to meet the requirements of employment and destiny. Or the destiny and employment urges may pull the person irresistibly in a certain direction, while the personality may lack the necessary enthusiasm and resources to fulfil that destiny. Recognising the conflict is halfway to solving the problem, and an objective party, armed with a numerological interpretation, may achieve a breakthrough in understanding. But there is also no reason why individuals could not use the numerological perspective to recognise their own conflicts.

Lack of harmony within the personality may surface in unsettled and unsuitable behaviour. People in guiding roles may develop strategies to address and neutralise these conflicts. This may help their clients or friends gain the personality strength they need to resolve their own dilemmas. Numerology could be one more tool in helping others in their personal healing process.

Numerology could be helpful in our work relationships. We may find ourselves being asked for advice by a friend who is having problems. Though we may feel confident in offering advice based on the knowledge gained from our own experiences, an interpretation of the Spheres of Influence revealed in a numerology chart may reveal a new perspective which may prove to be rewarding if acted upon.

It is said that "we choose our friends, but not our relatives". This statement may also be true of people we meet in the work place and with whom we may find ourselves in conflict. Numerology can show us how best to deal with these people to encourage a relationship of harmony rather than animosity. But the application of lessons gleaned from a numerological perspective will be able to do more than defuse potential conflict; it can also show how to recognise the assets of individuals and build on them if needed. People in supervisory and managerial positions will have invaluable assistance in choosing the right people for the right jobs.

A study of numerology will also describe the personality potential of a child and could give us guidance in the best directions to steer them to fulfil this apparent potential. Understanding the inherent nature of children through numerology may provide some answers as to why they behave in certain ways. If it is behaviour we do not wish to encourage, we may ask ourselves if we are imposing our personality on a child who is quite different from ourselves. If we analyse the personality differences between ourselves and our children and try to judge whether the desired behaviour is compatible with their personalities, a greater rapport will be established within the family. We may often set goals for our children which merely reflect our own unfulfilled ambitions. Numerology can help us to assess objectively whether their behaviour is really unacceptable and deserving of discipline and correction, or whether it is behaviour we are personally ill-equipped to understand and tolerate.

As children become more sophisticated as a result of the information age, they are demanding reasons for rules and are challenging why adults should have the controlling power in determining their welfare. If more of our decisions are based on numerological insights we may be able to encourage children to appreciate the numerological perspective we see and together we may concentrate on the most positive aspects of their potential, thereby nurturing welcome harmony in family relationships.

Teachers may find this book helpful in their dealings with their students. It can serve as a time-saving device for understanding their pupils and for choosing subjects for study. A child whose birth date shows mental orientation will have few manual skills and should be guided into academic subjects. Teachers may see why some students excel in particular subjects and others have to plod along. Numerology could assist them in choosing the right pupils for sporting, social and other cultural activities, while at the same time recognising the rights of those who do not wish to participate in a particular activity. If they complete a numerological interpretation of an apparently recalcitrant student they need to reach, they may well find the cause of a possible communication breakdown and modify aspects of their approach. In doing so, they may succeed in developing the rapport they seek.

A unique feature of this book is the very large number of

names listed alphabetically under their numerical value. There are many ways in which these lists could be used.

One significant way is to help choose a name for a baby. These lists are designed to give inspiration to expectant parents so that a long and often indecisive search for a suitable name may be avoided. As well as listing the names we expect to find, like Peter, John, Stephen, Sue, Anne and Margaret, it also features modern and unusual names — Jordana, Casey and Tara, Kyle, Lindell and Riordan. It has one of the longest lists of names to be found in any name book.

The female name list is also noticeably longer than the male. There appears to be a tradition for more female names to be created from one "basic" (root) name than for males. For example, over 40 derivatives can be created from Catherine — Caitlin, Cassy, Catarina, Cathlene, Cathy, Catie, Kitty — just to name a few. But, if we look at the male names with the greatest potential for manipulation, Richard or Michael for example, only about 20 names can be created.

This situation is compounded because today's parents are prepared to be more adventurous and experimental with female, rather than male names. A scan of the birth notices in metropolitan newspapers illustrates this point. Comparative lists of uncommon male and female baby names are most likely to show that the list of female names is twice the length of the male list.

Traditional name books have focused on the historical meanings taken from, among others, the Celtic, Anglo-Saxon, Scandinavian, Greek and Latin tongues. Many meanings also have religious significance. We are also seeing the emergence of new names, some of which are traditional names spelt differently or altered in some way. While new names obviously cannot have historical meanings, neither does it seem appropriate to apply historical meanings to names that have deliberately been changed from their traditional form.

We would like to be bold and suggest that while we may be curious about the historical meanings of names, this knowledge will not be useful to a child. However, if names are chosen with regard to their vibratory powers in relation to the birth date, there is every chance that the characteristics pertaining to the vibrations of the name will unfold in the child's personality.

The name, especially the given name, plays an important role in balancing and strengthening the features of the child's birth date. We will explain how parents can do their children a service by choosing a name which will have the best possible effect on a child's personality and destiny. From the large number of names provided, parents can prepare short lists of names with number values that would suit the anticipated birth date or dates.

Adults may peruse the lists and discover the suitability of their own names and those of others in relation to their birth dates. The lists could be used by someone contemplating a change of given name. Alternatively, they can help in the less complex but no less effective practice of changing the spelling of the existing given name. These lists feature names that have minor spelling changes but that also change their vibration and therefore their influence on an individual's personality and potential. This is an area we can explore with interest, but also with caution. A decision on a name change is not one to be made on the spur of the moment. Nevertheless, a change wisely undertaken can have worthwhile results.

The numbers of our birth dates and names are a mirror of our personality and destiny. Numerology interprets the fascinating interrelation of these numbers and describes the multidimensional facets of individuality and potential.

The chapters that follow are a step by step guide to how to develop the facility to obtain information through numbers and how to gain a good understanding of this information. We examine six principal Spheres of Influence which combine to form our personality complex. Two of these spheres are found in the birth date and four within the names. Once a good working knowledge of each of these spheres has been attained, the next step should be to acquire the skill to see them all at once. We cannot expect to immediately make wise decisions based on numerological insights. It takes time and experience to appreciate the complexity of the number combinations and to interpret their meaning accurately. However, with patience and enthusiasm we will gain many remarkable insights into personality and potential.

This book is designed for the general reader and is not a definitive textbook. Many intricate aspects of numerology have been intentionally omitted. For readers keen to develop further knowledge we recommend continued study accompanied by constant observation of the working of the various vibratory influences on themselves and others.

THE SIX SPHERES OF INFLUENCE

Before we can gain any significant wisdom from the lessons of numerology, we need to calculate the numbers which are to be the mirror to the personality, talents and destiny of the person or persons we wish to study. This section may be used as a quick reference to calculate the numbers or symbols of the Six Spheres of Influence.

As mentioned in the previous chapter, the symbols of numerology are the numbers 1 to 9. This means that any number beyond 9 needs to be reduced to a single digit to arrive at the numerological symbol of that number. This is done by simple addition. For example, 33 is $3 + 3 = 6$, or 19 is $1 + 9 = 10$ and $1 + 0 = 1$. The numerological symbols of 33 and 19 are 6 and 1 respectively.

Once the numerological symbol or final digit has been determined we consider its characteristics as well as the characteristics of the numbers that served to form this digit. There are two exceptions to this rule, however, and these are the multiple numbers 11 and 22. They are known as Master numbers and are not reduced to 2 and 4 respectively. More information on these Master numbers is given in Chapter 3.

THE BIRTH DATE
FIRST AND SECOND SPHERES OF INFLUENCE

FIRST SPHERE

The only important piece of information we need is the birth date. It is most important to know the correct date. Often, the year of birth is not readily known and hasty attempts are made to calculate the year. This is a risky practice which may lead to an incorrect finding of the Second Sphere of Influence. However, once the correct birth date is known we may record it as our first step. The following are examples of three different types of birth dates:

$$A — 7 . 5 . 1956$$

$$B — 17 . 2 . 1961$$
$$(8)$$

$$C — 22 . 1 . 1966$$

The First Sphere of Influence is formed and governed by the number or numbers of the *day* of birth. It indicates the kind of personality. In example **A** this sphere is wholly controlled by the single 7 vibration. Interpretation of this personality will rely heavily on the characteristics of this number. In example **B** we have a multiple birthday indicating that this sphere is controlled by a set of three vibrations. The 17 is reduced to 8, which makes this individual an Eight personality. However, the 1 and 7 vibrations will continue to operate, usually in the foreground of the personality, while the 8 vibration is active in the background. A careful examination of three interchanging and interpenetrating vibrations is required here. In example **C** the Master vibration 22 has control over this sphere. As will be explained in a later chapter, a Master number is considered as a unit and is not reduced to a single digit. The 22 in this case will not be reduced to 4 but interpreted in terms of the qualities and potential of the Master vibration. However, caution should be exercised in relating the individual to all these qualities as they are attained by very few, though the potential always remains to be used. The characteristics of the 4 vibration come into force when those of the 22 are not used.

SECOND SPHERE

To ascertain the governing number of this sphere we add up the numbers of the birth date and reach a total. This total, which is always a multiple number, is then reduced to a single digit which represents the Second Sphere of Influence. However, when the Master numbers 11 and 22 appear in the totals they are not reduced any further. The number of this Sphere of Influence is also known as our Destiny Number and plays a very significant role in our lives. Using the birth dates already mentioned we ascertain the numbers of this Second Sphere as follows:

7 . 5 . 1956 — 7 + 5 + 1 + 9 + 5 + 6 = 33 = **6**

17 . 2 . 1961 — 1 + 7 + 2 + 1 + 9 + 6 + 1 = 27 = **9**

22 . 1 . 1966 — 2 + 2 + 1 + 1 + 9 + 6 + 6 = 27 = **9**

In these examples the numbers 6, 9 and 9 respectively form the Second Sphere of Influence and represent the Destiny Numbers.

To avoid misinterpretation of this Sphere of Influence, short cuts should not be taken to calculate this number. A common mistake is to calculate the single digit of the birthday, month and year and then add these three numbers together. For example 17 . 2 . 1961 becomes 8 + 2 + 8 = 18 = 9. Though the final number is correct for this example, if any Master numbers are involved, the calculation may be wrong. For example, with the birth date 15 . 8 . 1961, the incorrect method would give us 6 + 8 + 8 = 22. The correct method is 1 + 5 + 8 + 1 + 9 + 6 + 1 = 31 = 4. This person does not have a 22 destiny. Furthermore, when a detailed study of numerology is undertaken it will be seen that the single digit 9 formed from the multiple 27 holds greater force than that formed from the multiple 18.

Having worked out the First and Second Spheres of Influence we may now present the birth dates as follows:

First Sphere	7 .	5 . 1956 = 33 = **6**	Second Sphere
First Sphere	17 . (8)	2 . 1961 = 27 = **9**	Second Sphere
First Sphere	22 .	1 . 1966 = 27 = **9**	Second Sphere

THE WHOLE NAME
THIRD, FOURTH, FIFTH AND SIXTH SPHERES OF INFLUENCE

The next step is to determine the four Spheres of Influence operating within the whole name — the whole name being the given name, the middle name or names, if any, and the surname. In order to do so we convert the letters of the whole name to their number values. Each letter of the alphabet has a corresponding numerical value, as shown in the following chart:

1	2	3	4	5	6	7	8	9
A	B	C	D	E	F	G	H	I
J	K	L	M	N	O	P	Q	R
S	T	U	V	W	X	Y	Z	

We shall use the name Tamerra Idelle Saunders to illustrate these spheres.

IMOGEN
94 6 755 36 = 9

THIRD SPHERE

The single digit resulting from the total of the number values of the letters of the given name is the emblem of this sphere.

T A M E R R A

2 1 4 5 9 9 1 — added across this totals 31 which is reduced to 4

The vibration number 4 operating from this sphere will play a positive, negative or neutral role in influencing Tamerra's personality and talents.

IMOGEN CYNTHIA WHYTE
946755 3752891 58725
9   8   9

FOURTH SPHERE

The single digit resulting from the total of the number values of the letters of the whole name is the emblem of this sphere.

T A M E R R A   I D E L L E   S A U N D E R S

2 1 4 5 9 9 1	9 4 5 3 3 5	1 1 3 5 4 5 9 1	
31	29	29	
4	11	11	
4 +	2 +	2	= 8

The numbers of each letter of each name are added across and the totals reduced to single digits. These digits are then added to arrive at the final total. The number 8 resulting from this method of calculation is the clue to this person's natural talents and aptitudes which can be applied to a career and leisure activities.

17 · 9 + 8 · 9
26 = 8

FIFTH SPHERE

The single digit resulting from the total of the number values of the vowels of the whole name is the emblem of this sphere:

TAMERRA IDELLE SAUNDERS

T	A	M	E	R	R	A		I	D	E	L	L	E		S	A	U	N	D	E	R	S
1		5		1	9	5		5			1	3			5							
		7								19								9				
		7								10								9				
		7				+				1				+				9			= 17 = 8	

Tamerra's inner person will be motivated by the characteristics of the 8 vibration.

SIXTH SPHERE

The single digit resulting from the total of the number values of the consonants of the whole name is the emblem of this sphere.

T	A	M	E	R	R	A		I	D	E	L	L	E		S	A	U	N	D	E	R	S
2		4		9	9				4		3	3			1			5	4		9	1
		24								10								20				
		6				+				1				+				2			= 9	

Tamerra's outer personality will display the qualities of the 9 vibration.

If the Master numbers 11 and 22 appear in the final total they should not be reduced further, but recorded and interpreted as such. If they appear in subtotals they need not be taken into consideration. At the same time, we should remember that people do not consistently live up to the power of these master vibrations, and they automatically revert to the influences of the straightforward 2 or 4 vibrations. Two interpretations will therefore be advisable.

INTERPRETATION OF SPHERES

The First Sphere of Influence is established on the day we are born and gives us a particular personality type, which is further strengthened or weakened by the numbers of the birth month and year and by the vibrations of the given name — the Third Sphere of Influence. Several powerful forces combine to form this First Sphere. Success in all our endeavours will depend on the compatibility and cooperation of our personality type with the other Spheres of Influence. As this is our stamp of individuality, it may be regarded as the most important sphere. The only factor that can, to a degree, inhibit or enhance our personality traits will be overriding influences of our environment.

This First Sphere is temporarily obscured in our casual meetings. On these occasions people encounter the forces of the Sixth Sphere of Influence — the outer person. These forces are not always the same as those forming our essential personality type and may give faulty first impressions. The Sixth Sphere can be consciously and unconsciously used to enhance personal traits of the First Sphere and advance the prospects of the Second Sphere of Destiny. It could also be used to conceal and deceive as the Sixth Sphere is the facade and not the true person. If the same vibration controls the first, fifth and sixth spheres, the individual will in fact be exactly what he or she appears to be. This is more the exception than the rule.

The Second Sphere of Influence which controls our destiny is often referred to as our Life Path. There is a constant draw of the personality towards the requirements of this sphere. If the personality type formed by the First Sphere is in overall sympathy with the demands of the destiny, little or no difficulty will be found and a downstream journey through life can be expected. However, if these two vital spheres are controlled by vibrations of conflicting natures, many adjustments within both spheres will be needed before fulfilment is achieved.

For an instant numerological assessment of a person, the First and Second Spheres can suffice to obtain considerable insight into the personality and destiny. Furthermore, the birth date needed for determining these spheres is always readily available and the only mental calculation needed is the reduction of the numbers of the birth date to a single digit.

The Third Sphere of Influence can intentionally be used as a powerful means of influencing all other spheres. It can be used to introduce a balancing vibration found wanting in the birth date. It can be used as a connecting link between the first and second spheres to enhance the power of a particular talent and to promote the chances of fulfilling the requirements of destiny. To the degree that we are conscious of the influence of our given names upon our personality, to that degree will the power of its vibrations assist us. This is the secret of its success. This principle also applies to the effectiveness of the numbers of all other spheres.

Returning to the Sixth Sphere of Influence, the outer person, we would like to stress that, though its impact is only of a temporary nature, it is nevertheless a permanent aspect of our personality. All our first impressions are created and gained through this sphere. It takes over in order of importance whenever we meet people for the first time. It is our prime asset at interviews of any sort. The need to constantly emphasise the positive qualities of this sphere and eliminate the negative ones cannot be overemphasised. An unimpressive and untidy outer personality projected through this sphere could do grave injustice to a splendid real personality. The reverse is also true.

The Fourth Sphere of Influence reveals the working talents we already possess and can be used in our professions and hobbies. Ideally, these talents will be able to meet the requirements of our destiny and will not conflict with our personality type. If they are in conflict, new talents may have to be developed in order to fulfil our destiny and our existing talents be used for secondary purposes. This is not uncommon.

The Fifth Sphere of Influence, or inner person, generally plays a concealed role as the combined forces of the other spheres and environmental influences may commit it to the background. However, the forces of this sphere do not remain in this position permanently. They emerge from time to time to influence our behaviour in long-term affairs, and for this reason it is essential that this sphere is examined whenever longer term associations are envisaged.

The single significant fact that emerges from this brief examination of the six spheres is their interdependence. Their interdependence is not surprising as the human personality needs to function as a well-balanced whole in order to fulfil itself by answering the call of destiny and making a worthwhile contribution to society. All six spheres must therefore be examined for a balanced interpretation of the integral personality and the degree of influence each sphere has in forming this whole. There is an important numerological fact that needs to be considered when examining these spheres. The unique characteristics of the numbers will remain constant, regardless of the sphere in which they appear, but they will express themselves differently according to their position in the birth date and the whole name.

The two Spheres of Influence within the birth date take precedence over those of the whole name as the birth date is fixed and comprises the mould in which an individual is formed by the vibrations or cosmic forces prevailing on the day of birth. However, the whole name determines the nature of the four other spheres and, by contrast, they are not fixed. Parents have a choice before the birth of a child as to its given and middle names (sometimes the surname too). Adults may choose to change their given and middle names unofficially, or if by deed poll, they may also include their surname.

In a numerological analysis, it is the given name that

takes the highest priority and it is on this Third Sphere of Influence that this book concentrates. The vibration of the given name has a direct bearing on the First and Second Spheres and its influence can add harmony or conflict to the personality. It also contributes, along with the other names, towards forming the Fourth, Fifth and Sixth Spheres of Influence.

An assessment of the numbers of all six Spheres of Influence provides a fascinating amalgam of abilities, attitudes, ambitions, potential, emotions and conflicts. Numbers may be compatible and bring harmony, or in conflict and cause divisions within the personality. Other numbers may add strength to the harmony, or divisions. Some numbers may neutralise each other, while the power of others may be simply submerged. While our ultimate aim should be to gain the ability to see all six spheres at once, it is advisable to concentrate on the relative significance of each sphere and the circumstances in which one or more, at certain times, takes precedence over others. Eventually, we will realise the nature of an astonishing phenomenon held together in an elusive form which we call the personality complex.

The web of our life is of a mingled yarn, good and ill together.

Change "life" to "personality" in this quotation from Shakespeare and it summarises the complex interrelation of the spheres.

THE FIRST SPHERE OF INFLUENCE
THE NUMBER OR NUMBERS OF THE BIRTHDAY

In terms of strength and influence, the number or numbers of the day of birth are the most significant. These numbers or vibrations form the personality type and may be seen as the First Sphere of Influence. Someone born on the 7th day of any month will possess the properties of the 7 vibration and may be regarded, by and large, as a Seven personality. However, a multiple-digit birthday such as the 25th will also produce a Seven personality, but this individual will not be a straightforward Seven as the 2 and 5 vibrations will constantly influence the basic 7 vibration. A correct assessment of this birthday will include the interpretation of a set of three vibrations. For the most part, the 2 and 5 vibrations will operate in the forefront of the personality while the underlying 7 will be active in the background. In other words, in a single-digit birthday, personal characteristics are concentrated and in a multiple-digit birthday they are distributed, forming a complex personality.

Some degree of caution and skill is needed to interpret a multiple-numbered birthday owing to the constant interplay of three equally strong vibrations. After careful analysis a person may begin to appreciate which aspects of their personality are influenced by which particular number in their birthday. Some aspects of a person's personality may be compounded because the numbers could be multiplying the influence of specific characteristics. For example, the 1, 7 and 8 vibrations of someone whose birthday falls on the 17th day of a month impart a tendency towards intolerance and it therefore becomes a trait which needs strict management to control its implications. Any similarities between specific aspects of numbers in a multiple-digit birthday should be looked for and it should be recognised that the repetition of traits and the multiple appearance of the same number in a birth date will multiply the strength of their influence.

In this chapter each number or vibration is examined with comments on general personality traits, positive and negative characteristics, descriptions of a personality's behaviour in social situations and relationships, the method of handling money, some career prospects and an analysis of children of each personality type. There is also general information on fashion, style, harmonious colours, gems and best days for business.

VIBRATION NUMBER 1
Letters A, J, S

The number 1 vibration is the active part of the two primeval vibrations. It represents beginning, especially of physical life, and is consequently the prime mover or the motivator of all other vibrations. It is the only number that determines whether personality traits are used in a positive or negative manner. The degree in which positive and negative qualities will be active depends on the frequency of this number appearing in the birth date and names. Its influence on the personality is modified by the presence of other numbers. On the other hand, the absence of other numbers, leaving an abundance of the number 1, can increase the strength of this vibration considerably in a powerful and positive way. However, there is a point where the dominance of this number turns an individual to negative forms of expression. More information on the 1 vibration's influence is given in Chapter 5, under the heading Negativity.

Positive personalities with this vibration display individuality as their most distinguishing characteristic. This is because the number 1 represents the first vibration, which has known no other condition. These people cannot follow or emulate, but can only generate from within themselves. They are also known for many other correlative qualities, such as independence, self-reliance, leadership, inventiveness, ambition, authority, determination, courage, vital energy, and loyalty. The pronouns "I", "me" or "my" are constantly used in thought and speech and reflect their general "me first" and "me only" attitudes.

There are several other attributes unique to this number, such as concentration, ability to work under stress, quick recuperative powers after illness, a pragmatic approach to life, a long memory and strong opinions. This primeval vibration produces the genuine nonconformist. Those influenced strongly by it are rigid in their down-to-earth views, especially if supported by a 4 vibration. They do not stand out as conversationalists but enjoy person-to-person communication on subjects of their own choice in which their activities and interests figure largely. They are self-opinionated though not always well informed. They would instantly withdraw from the frivolous general conversation of a large group. The power of the 1 vibration is contained within the written word rather than the spoken word. They experience no difficulty in gathering a personal following, or having their ideas copied or followed by others. They expect others to defer to them and may display agitation and even ill-temper if this is not done. Vanity and self-esteem make them bad losers and extremely sensitive to criticism and contradiction. A subtle approach rather than a head-on confrontation should be used with these personalities. They get on best with Two, Four, Seven and Eight personalities.

There are some characteristics that are found wanting in these personalities; these include adaptability, ease in oral expression, emotional demonstration, cooperation, flexibility, tact, patience and humility. They simply refuse to admit an error on their part and may go to absurd lengths to justify their words and actions. Two other things they find difficult to do are to listen to others and to laugh at themselves.

Negative qualities common to this vibration are excess of ego, boastfulness, pride, ill-temper, impatience, vanity, narrow-mindedness, obstinacy, dictatorship, self-centredness and indecision. Conversation is excessively centred on self and self-interests. If not softened by a more flexible number, these people could live in the extremes of a black and white world without the ability to steer a middle course.

One personalities establish financial security early in life by their good sense of values. As they do not enjoy "luck" in the generally accepted way, they make their own. Gold is another important symbol of this vibration, and not only is it a desirable colour for its subjects, but they actively seek and get the things in life that this metal can obtain.

Motivated strongly by a physical vibration, Ones are sensitive to their physical environment and do not hesitate to spend their resources on personal luxuries. At the same time, they are discriminating buyers who are not prompted by impulse. Extraordinary satisfaction and pride is derived by them from a sense of ownership. They will be the quickest to pay off loans taken for the purchase of property and other goods.

In public life they succeed and thrive in positions demanding leadership, originality, initiative, independence and freedom of decision making. They are at their best in positions of authority or in self-employment. They function poorly as subordinates as they resent interference and would rather give orders than receive them. In all other affairs, too, they are givers rather than receivers. As the primeval vibration concerned with outgoing tendencies, the law of attraction and receiving is still inoperative. Subjects of this vibration therefore are still unaware of this opposite force which becomes operative with the number 2. Consequently, they are happier when they acquire their needs entirely through their own efforts. They do not like being placed under obligation to others by receiving favours and gifts.

Owing to the natural tendency of One personalities towards decision making, they should avoid equal partnerships since the balance and cooperation needed in such situations will be upset. They work with concentration and intensity and greatly resent interference and disturbance.

As companions they naturally take the leading role and could be quite demanding without realising it. Their habit of intense concentration not only makes them oblivious of their surroundings but also creates a stern facial expression. Consequently, they appear to be indifferent to their surroundings. This is, in fact, not true. It may take some time to understand that they are not intentionally shutting out those around them and that this habit of concentration and single-mindedness is a natural part of their individuality and contains no hostility.

They are loyal and protective marriage partners who will fight hard to save a marriage faced with problems. They will not easily surrender the responsibility of a commitment, especially one of marriage and family. Separation and divorce are not situations usually considered as solutions. Natural self-restraint and poor emotional expression make them unromantic partners, though their love is deep and abiding. They are not flirtatious and will consequently not tolerate competition in the field of love and affection. Their love and devotion are displayed by deeds rather than smooth talk.

Their partners need to be compromising, unselfish, patient and devoted. These qualities in the domestic scene are needed by One personalities as a back-up for their activities in the material world. They are strongly resentful of demanding companions. They are dependable providers and maintain firmly the role of head of the family, while demanding loyalty and love in return. This latter position of controlling member is assumed regardless of their position as either the wage earner or homemaker.

An insult or injury to a member of the family by an outsider will rarely be forgotten or forgiven. They are totally devoted to the welfare of their offspring and their partners are often obliged to take second place. Their long memories are used both in positive and negative ways, not only in family affairs but in all other activities. Although the strongest possible support is given to their families, they are career people rather than domesticated ones. Extreme restlessness will be experienced if they are confined by circumstances to family and domestic duties.

The best partners for these people will be those strongly influenced by the 2 vibration. Such a partnership will provide a good balance of active and receptive contributions, as the 2 is the receptive part of the primeval vibrations.

As children, One personalities will display the typical 1 qualities of independence, will-power, determination, individuality, self-reliance and leadership. Parents and guardians should recognise and appreciate these traits, as well as the creative mental activity of such children, and provide them with opportunities to develop along lines that will give full expression to their creative talents.

Family and social restrictions may inhibit these children during vital years of growth and force them into negative avenues of expression, such as insubordination, obstinacy, introversion, poor oral expression and as leaders in antisocial activities. They could be resentful of correction, domineering, uncooperative and rough in speech and manner. Fear of losing their individuality may bring about a lack of consideration for others. They should be encouraged, on the one hand, to maintain their individuality and on the other hand they should be shown that it is possible to sublimate ego in selfless group service for the good of all. In other words, to maintain individuality within group activity.

These children are quite capable of going their own way and standing on their own feet early in life. They are the quickest to recover from the trauma of a broken home and will be the first to take over responsibility of younger children and even become the new providers. They usually leave home early, even from a well-established one, due to their spirit of independence and adventure. Family loyalty, however, will always remain strong.

The best days for One personalities to transact business are Sundays and Mondays, especially if these days fall on the 1st, 10th, 19th or 28th of any month. On these days the vibratory make-up of these personalities and the vibrations prevailing will be in harmony.

The 1 vibration symbolises the sun, whose golden rays have a powerful influence on all One personalities and it accounts for their extraordinary love of sunshine. The colours most suitable and desirable in their dress and surroundings are, not surprisingly, gold, yellow, bronze, golden browns, copper, apricot, flame, orange and all colours of autumn. The best stones to be used by them are topaz (yellow), turquoise, amber, ruby and other stones of these colours. All their jewels should be set in gold.

People born on the 1st and 10th may regard themselves as straightforward One personalities. Those born on the 19th are also strong One personalities with this vibration operating in the foreground as well as the background of the personality. However, the personality will be heavily tempered by the power of the 9 vibration. This is regarded as a very advantageous birthday. The 28th also produces One personalities with little or no conflict between the three vibrations which control the personality. Many of the One qualities are tempered by the Two and others enhanced by the powerful 8.

The 1 vibration also appears in the birth dates 11th, 12th, 13th, 14th, 15th, 16th, 17th, 18th, 21st, 29th and 31st. Although these days do not produce One personalities, the influence of the 1 vibration is strong and many of its characteristics should be taken into consideration, especially those of self-confidence and leadership.

VIBRATION NUMBER 2
Letters B, K, T

The 1 vibration on its own is incomplete and unproductive until it is polarised into equal forces. This division results in the forming of active and receptive vibrations, and their subsequent interaction is the basis of all creation. The number 2 symbolises the receptive pole.

While motivation and action are the basic forces of the 1,

receptivity and conservation of power form the nature of the 2 vibration. Whereas the 1 represents individuality, the 2 represents associations, partnerships and union. In more basic terms, the 1 vibration stands for the principle of the provider and the 2 stands for the principle of the keeper.

Two personalities, although concerned with self, are always ready to sacrifice time and energy for the welfare and happiness of others. This sacrifice, nevertheless, demands an equal response in the form of attention and appreciation. The self-centredness of the 1, or the "me first" attitude, exists in the Twos as well and is displayed in their need for constant attention. The 2 is, however, a fluid vibration with the added qualities of emotion and awareness, and Two personalities are able to extend themselves out of self-centredness and see the needs of others and give understanding, support and comfort. People do not hesitate to confide in them for they are seen as being warm and sympathetic.

Some of the positive qualities of the 2 vibration include gentleness, persuasion, patience, impartiality, tact, diplomacy, self-sacrifice, unselfishness, romanticism, gallantry, charm, courtesy, consideration, grace and, above all, cooperation. People with a Two personality are persuasive rather than aggressive and can tone down aggressiveness in others by their gentle approach. In the Book of Proverbs it is said: "A soft answer turneth away wrath." This is usually the typical reaction of these personalities. They are known for their winning ways and their refined and genteel natures. They often obscure the great strength of character they possess by frequently misleading others into assuming they are weak-willed. They express their opinions in a roundabout manner and often say one thing and mean another: they resent being cornered into giving a firm opinion. Most people are attracted to Two personalities and they have an aura that frequently draws gifts and offers of help from others — benefits for which subjects of other aggressive vibrations have to work. They are the true gatherers, not only of physical things but also of facts and figures. It is very seldom that a Two personality will not be a collector of something or other.

All Two personalities possess a powerful imagination which is more whimsical than creative. They are also known for their psychic ability and extrasensory perception, unless these gifts have been suppressed in their upbringing. This is a noncompetitive vibration, and Two personalities are more concerned with participation than winning. The strongest desire of all Twos is for a peaceful lifestyle. If they do not find this they will withdraw into a private world of fantasy. In order to bring out their best qualities, they need a harmonious and peaceful atmosphere, whether in the domestic scene or elsewhere. They are instantly inhibited by disharmony. Their nervous systems are easily damaged by a life filled with discord, tension, uncleanliness and ugliness.

While the sun symbolises the 1 vibration and influences its subjects, the moon is the symbol of the 2 vibration and individuals strongly influenced by this number have their moods attuned to the phases of the moon. They are generally "night" people who make sure they have a good "sleep-in" the following day.

Twos are neither individualists nor loners — as their One counterparts. They are extroverts who need social life and company. Those strongly subject to this vibration may appear to be slightly lost or dreamy in aspect. They are not solo performers and feel more comfortable being part of a group. They prefer to remain on the fringe of activity, rather than become the centre of attention. They relate better with those who are younger or older than themselves. They are too sensitive to keep up with the pressure of handling their contemporaries. Close and long-term friendships are found within this vibration. Many Twos turn out to be lasting pen-friends. These personalities get on best with Ones, Sevens, Fours and Eights.

Average Two personalities need more self-assertiveness, self-confidence, objectivity, logic and independence. They could be manipulated by unscrupulous people and are more inclined to imitate others instead of daring to be themselves. They show a dislike for argument and will go to great lengths to avoid such situations, even to the extent of subordinating and compromising their own views.

The 2 vibration has its negative traits too. They are: uncertainty, changeability, oversensitivity, self-consciousness, self-deprecation, timidity, fear of opinions, fear of failure, procrastination, shyness, indecision, depression, hypochondria, loneliness and emotional overreaction.

Financial security is important to the well-being of Two personalities, but this must be provided by others as the Twos do not adopt a persistent course in the pursuit of financial gain. They are generous with their money and enjoy giving gifts as much as they enjoy receiving tokens of affection.

These personalities work best as partners, as seconds-in-charge, and as deputies and subordinates. Their talents are displayed while assisting, cooperating and carrying out the plans of others rather than originating and directing. They are not meant for manual labour and are in their element in occupations where movement is involved, such as travel and communication. Most Twos have a natural urge to follow some form of medical or healing practice. They are also successful in any job that requires precision and delicacy of touch.

People with a Two personality fall in love easily. They make excellent marriage partners, provided they are not negative Twos. The type of negativity produced by the 2 vibration can make these personalities quite burdensome. The average Two is prepared to play a back-up role in marriage and is best married to an assertive personality or one controlled by active vibrations. A domestic life free from tension and financial worries is essential. Without romance and variety in marriage they could be tempted to look elsewhere, especially if they do not receive the constant love and attention they need. There is a waywardness in the emotional life of Twos. They are easily won over by consideration and other romantic approaches such as frequent, but not necessarily costly, tokens of affection. Partners of these people who recognise this need and pander to their sentimental natures receive a good deal in return. Given love and security, they could be towers of strength to their partners, as the strength of the Two will flourish only in these circumstances. Maternal instinct is strong and all others under the Twos' influence will receive this mothering.

Children with a Two personality will display a strong adverse reaction to noise or a discordant and inharmonious environment. They enjoy living in a fantasy world of their own and this pastime may be carried well into adulthood. Sensitivity and shyness will always be problems, especially in their rough and tumble school days. Peace and harmony at home is vital for the development of these children. They can easily develop a variety of strange inhibitions and complexes under callous and neglectful treatment by parents, guardians and older brothers and sisters. These complexes could remain as serious personality problems as they mature into adults. They are home-living and gentle natured and need the society of children of their own refined manners. These children may suffer adversely from the result of a broken home and the events that led up to it. They are sentimental and cry easily as an outlet for their emotions.

These children are non-aggressive and should not be pushed into strongly competitive sport. Owing to the natural rhythm in their bodies and minds, they take to swimming, dancing, acrobatics and any other sport where rhythmic and fluid movements are essential. They are true water babies and their natural love of water, especially the sea and other large expanses of water, will remain all their lives. There will be more Two personalities in the navies of the world than in any of the other armed services. The 2 vibration's talent for the written word will be seen in these children at an early stage.

It must be recognised that these children have great depth of talent and goodness, which will blossom only in the right environment. Corporal punishment, even of the mildest sort, will have unfortunate and lasting effects on them.

The best days for Two personalities to transact business are Sundays, Mondays and Fridays, especially if they fall on the 2nd, 11th, 20th or 29th of any month.

Genuine Two personalities look and feel their best in soft, flowing clothes. Strict business suits are not their style, neither are loud and showy fabrics and designs. Pale colours are most suitable in dress and surroundings. White and lighter shades of green, cream, salmon, blue and aquamarine should be used. Dark colours should be avoided. Their stones are pearls, moonstones and pale green stones set in silver.

People born on the 2nd and 20th are true Two person-alities, while those born on the 11th and 29th revert to the influence of the 2 vibration if they do not keep up with the high octaves of the master number 11. Although not producing straightforward Two personalities, this vibration also influences significantly those persons born on the 12th and 21st to 28th of any month.

VIBRATION NUMBER 3
Letters C, L, U

The fusion of the active 1 and receptive 2 vibrations brings forth a third which is symbolised by the number 3. This new vibration stands for the principle of youth, possessing inherited traits of its parentage as well as distinct qualities of its own, thus giving it a much wider range of motivation and expression. It is the first vibration that contains a mixture of both active and recep-tive attributes, but with the active elements predominating.

It is an extrovert vibration and, true to its youthful nature, the zest for living and self-expression are the dominant forces governing those strongly influenced by it. Concern for self and self-interests are prominent features, as in the case of the

One and Two personalities. This is the third vibration of the self-centred trio.

People with this vibration shaping their personalities have many endearing qualities, such as good manners, tact, charm, effervescence, vitality, enthusiasm, optimism, ambition, gaiety, generosity, loyalty, leadership, authority and, above all, versatility.

The most joyful of all personalities will usually be subjects of this vibration. Their eternal youthfulness, vitality, lack of oral frustration and easy self-expression give them greater opportunities for extracting pleasure out of life. This engaging lifestyle keeps them looking younger than their actual years.

Threes are subjects of the first vibration on the mental plane and are gifted with exceptionally high intelligence and an acute sense of accuracy. They insist on accuracy in their own performance as well as in others and can become irritated when others do not measure up to their standards. The negative ones go to extremes in this regard.

All Three personalities possess high artistic talent with a fine sense of colour and a keen appreciation of beauty in all things. A super imagination combined with creative thinking, inherited from the 1 vibration, make them the true creative artists. Some of their greatest pleasures are derived from creating beautiful things. Their need for artistic expression is shown in every field of activity in which they are engaged. For instance, if they take to the culinary arts, they will invariably turn to the decorative and creative aspects of this profession.

Excellence of speech, including quality of voice, is another outstanding feature of these personalities. The spoken word is their forte. They are lively and interesting conversationalists and natural entertainers, known for their sense of humour and repartee. As genuine extroverts they can be depended upon to lift the atmosphere of a group or party by their effervescence. However, they are sometimes in danger of talking too much and spoiling much of the good cheer they spread around.

Average Three personalities may suffer from certain drawbacks, such as the lack of practicality and pragmatism, the tendency to lose interest in a venture before it is completed, the habit of changing courses of study or careers before they have been successfuly established, and the lack of long-term planning of their future. Their versatility urges them to take up new challenges before they have attended to matters in hand. This usually results in the scattering of their talents if they are not well advised and directed, especially in the early stages of their careers. Centralisation of purpose and activity is needed on account of their frequent reluctance to harness their talents and use them towards specific ends.

On the negative side of this vibration, Three personalities may suffer from immaturity, irresponsibility, instability, inconsistency, extreme self-centredness, self-indulgence, fickleness, extravagance, intolerance, self-pity, meticulousness and megalomania. Although generally weak charactered they have an overbearing and pompous manner. Though seldom well informed, they are always strongly self-opinionated, a characteristic inherited from the 1.

All Threes, whether positive or negative or in between, are big spenders. Saving money is alien to their nature; they do not feel the need to provide for "rainy days" and are not depressed when their finances are low. Their sense of values is not focused on the accumulation of money but on the pleasure of using it. Their innate optimism overcomes fear of failure and fear of the future.

They are happiest working in company and are at their best in areas where they can set their own routine. They are quite capable of doing more than one thing at a time. They are usually unhappy in subordinate positions for they possess the inherited leadership qualities of the 1 vibration, though tempered by the tact and courtesy of the 2. They are original and creative rather than practical and mercenary. They excel in all ceremonial undertakings, whether religious, political, legal, military or social.

The surest way to get along with these people is to boost their egos. The negative ones accept this as a desperate and unconcealed need, while the positive ones take it in with subtlety and grace. On the other hand, a certain way to incur their displeasure is to fail to show them the respect they seem to regard as their due.

They have great need for the love and attention of the opposite sex. The negative Threes will perform extraordinary feats in order to draw this attention to themselves. However, the average Three has no need to do so, because of their charm, courtesy and popularity. These personalities get on best with Sixes and Nines. Their emotional lives will always be eventful, involving several affairs of the heart. Their feelings are easily hurt for they possess the sentimentality and emotionalism of the 2 vibration, though these traits are well concealed behind their extroverted natures.

Whereas the romanticism of the Two personality is of a

passive nature, that of the Three is self-initiated and active. They are flirtatious, but loyal and delightful companions with partners who can provide the admiration and affection they need and who can share their variety of interests. They are easily bored and may lose interest in a relationship that does not meet their needs.

Being one of the egocentric trio, these people concentrate on the joy of living according to their own standards and within their own interests. However, they are capable of remarkable self-sacrifice for a loved one in need of their devotion. Love is the one force that will draw them out of their self-interest. They are not domesticated people and will perform domestic chores only through necessity. Careers and social involvement are far more attractive to them.

The high intelligence of Three children may not always be displayed early. Their powerful imagination and lack of practicality keep their minds constantly wandering from one thing to another. They live in a dream world and are often accused of being scatterbrained. This condition, if it exists, is only a passing phase, for these are children with fertile minds who will handle their studies with ease. They grasp facts quickly and find no need to "burn the midnight oil" in order to keep up with their peers. Their vocabulary will develop early and remain above average.

A noticeable trait with these children is their good manners. This natural courtesy remains throughout their adult lives. They excel in a variety of sport but will not remain involved in body contact sports for long. They will always enjoy healthy competition and most amateurs are found in this vibration. Fierce loyalty to their friends may appear at times to be given at the expense of family loyalty. This is in fact not the case, for these children possess the capacity to handle their obligations to both friends and family. It must be accepted by parents and guardians that children with a three personality cannot be kept away from frequent social contact as this is part of their development. A happy family atmosphere with strict guidance is needed to prevent them from wasting their talents. They are not practical and will usually have trouble with timetables and routine duties. Their enthusiasm, imagination and gift of speech should be constantly encouraged.

The best days for Three personalities to transact business of any sort will be Sundays, Mondays and Fridays, especially if these days fall on the 3rd, 12th, 21st or 30th of any month.

These personalities are usually leaders in fashion. They

may design their own garments and are fond of bright colours and flamboyant styles. They are attracted to uniforms and do justice to them, as well as to the insignia and decorations that go with them. The colours that blend with their personalities are mauve, violet, purple, blue, crimson, rose, ruby and amber. Their precious stones are the amethyst and turquoise.

The 3rd and 30th days of any month, as well as the 12th and 21st, produce Three personalities. While individuals born on the 3rd and 30th have unmixed 3 characteristics, they will need the 1 vibration in a degree of strength in the rest of their birth dates or names in order to keep on the positive side of this vibration. Those with the 12th and 21st as their birthdays are already positive personalities and will be able to develop the best 3 qualities lying in the background of their personalities.

VIBRATION NUMBER 4
Letters D, M, V

Interaction between the 1, 2 and 3 vibrations produces the stable and earthly vibration represented by the number 4. Its earthly nature is the result of the influence of the planet Earth. As the strongest physical vibration, it stands for the establishment of a solid foundation for the material and physical aspects of life. It is a receptive and passive vibration. While the number 1 gives birth to an idea, the 2 gathers facts and figures pertaining to the idea, the 3 enhances and expands the concept, adding its touch of beauty and artistry, the 4 brings the whole concept down to earth and puts it into form. It is thus the vibration that produces the doer, the worker and the builder. The mind of the Four personality is focused along constructive lines on the physical plane.

The 4 vibration, not surprisingly, gives its subjects a pragmatic approach to life. Other qualities of this practical vibration are sturdiness, trustworthiness, reliability, prudence, judgement, loyalty, patriotism, persistence, orderliness, concentration, thrift and sincerity.

Other general characteristics that distinguish Fours from others are: dedication to work, proficiency with their hands as well as with their bodies, sensitivity to physical conditions, sound judgement, orderliness, self-discipline, calmness and good health. They are conservative in thought and action and usually resist change in their lifestyle. Many of them may run the risk of falling into a rut. The true "Doubting Thomas" comes from this vibration, especially in regard to abstract ideas and conceptions. They demand proof and value more than the subjects of any other vibration.

Fours have healthy appetites and are able to consume large quantities of food at a time. If a 6 vibration exists in the birth date as well, these people are likely to have problems with weight. The 6 vibration usually makes its subjects connoisseurs of food and wine.

Fours find great contentment when they are making or mending something. They are invariably called upon for help by less practical people and usually give much more than they receive for their labour. Working to excess, with little or no time left for play and recreation, could be an ever-present problem. Seldom do they show interest in esoteric studies. Religious practices are confined to the established order. In their interpretations of life's varied activities, rules and responsibilities, they are more inclined to follow the letter rather than the spirit of the law.

Fours need to be dealt with in a precise manner. The surest way to upset them is to indulge in generalisations. Patriotism, fondness of traditional ways of life, strong opinions of right and wrong, are other distinguishing traits. Their sense of humour is found in the form of practical jokes and situation comedy. They are mildly extroverted people whose conversation is neither imaginative nor lively but confined to practical considerations. They can be deeply hurt if boredom or condescension is shown by listeners on the infrequent occasions they decide to speak out. Four personalities get on best with other Fours, Ones, Twos and Eights.

Some desirable qualities lacking in the average Four personality are imagination, adaptability, flexibility, ambition, breadth of vision, inspiration, sentimentality, tact and adventure. They are unable to cope with emergencies, or to relax. These personalities possess to a greater degree the Twos' capacity to see more than one side of an issue but do not share their dislike of controversy and argument. On the contrary, Fours have an extraordinary and even aggravating habit of refusing to concede another's point of view, even when they can see its validity. They immediately take up an opposite viewpoint and argue stubbornly. This refusal to concede a point gains them a reputation for being contrary and dogmatic.

All vibrations, like the moon, have a dark side to their nature and this is referred to as their negative aspects. Such aspects common to the 4 vibration include pride, stubbornness, overexactness, fixity of opinions, dullness, stupidity, sloth, vulgarity, laziness, passivity, crudeness, meanness, clumsiness and selfishness. These are characteristics of the weak-minded, passive Fours. There are also negative Fours who are quite aggressive. These are easily distinguished by their destructiveness, rebellion, dogmatism, violence, cruelty, jealousy, intolerance, bigotry, dominance and greed. They are also excessively disciplinary towards others.

Financial security is constantly sought after by these people. They do not gamble but seek to acquire money and material possessions by hard work, sound judgement as to the value of acquisitions, and by driving hard bargains. A travelling salesperson will find it extremely difficult to sell anything of doubtful value or quality to homemakers ruled by this vibration. They will not be carried away by impulse or hurried into making a decision. They are thrifty and always have a nest-egg set aside. The negative ones could be niggardly. This is one of the safest vibrations for the management of money and other financial and property assets.

Fours are drawn into areas of work where dexterity with their hands and bodies could be used to full advantage. They usually work behind the scenes and are not adventurous in business. They rarely change jobs and interests. More gold watches are awarded for long service to these people than to those of other numbers. The close affinity of the vibration with the earth produces farmers, miners, geologists, surveyors, draughtsmen and workers in any occupation connected with the land. The exactitude that comes with the 4 makes them good accountants, auditors, estimators and economists. They have a keen sense of touch which enables them to produce wonderful physical forms in the world of art, such as sculptures, pottery, carvings and embroideries and similar creations. They can also excel as masons, surgeons and healers, or in any activity where the sense of touch is important.

Display of emotion is not natural to these physically oriented personalities. They are often embarrassed by displays of sentiment. Their love is shown by deeds and duty well performed rather than by words and demonstration of emotion. They are not too different to their One counterparts in this regard. As marriage partners they are totally loyal but unromantic and austere. There is a constant need for romance and imagination to be brought into their personal lives. They can be depended upon to provide a stable and financially secure home, though little or no interest will be taken in beautifying the home. They are inclined to exercise stern discipline within the family circle and they do this by setting an example. Negative Fours could take their disciplinary measures to excess.

Four children are usually healthy, physically strong and emotionally stable, though undemonstrative. They are quiet-spoken and lack fluency in speech. The negative ones could be stubborn, bullying, and may even exhibit a streak of cruelty. These children are not fierce competitors but their strength of purpose often brings them success over their less determined peers. They excel in body contact sports.

They can be relied upon from an early age to help around the home and gladly take responsibility for younger members of the family. Their native sturdiness provides comfort and strength in the event of a family break up. It is not in their nature to stray away from home. They like to save money, and this tendency will be noticed early in their cautious handling of pocket money.

Their education should be channelled into practical pursuits such as mechanics, technology, engineering, carpentry, or any field that requires aptitude with their hands and the number 4's ability to recognise and put into practice the blue-prints provided by others. Their social involvement will be more in the background of activity. They should not be forced into participation in the foreground if disinclined to do so. Their valuable contribution to society will always be as indispensable workers and helpers behind the scenes.

The best days for Four people to transact business are Saturdays, Sundays and Mondays, especially if these days fall on the 4th, 13th, 22nd or 31st of any month.

They are conservative in their choice of clothes, and the colours they should choose are green, emerald, silver, maroon and grey. Their jewel is the sapphire.

People born on the 4th day of any month will be the outright Four personalities. Other Four personalities born on the 13th, 22nd and 31st will have qualifying vibrations.

As in the case of other outright personalities from the number 2 onwards, the outright Fours will need the number 1 in other areas to help them in positive motivation. People born on the 22nd have the potential to ascend to the power of this master vibration, but here again they need the assistance of the number 1. If they revert to the plain 4 vibration, they will still need the 1. Those born on the 13th and 31st are exceptionally gifted people. Not only have they positive attitudes but they are also gifted with a powerful imagination as well as aptitude with their hands.

VIBRATION NUMBER 5
Letters E, N, W

While building and consolidating a firm foundation for the material and physical aspects of life are the principal features of the 4 vibration, the 5 takes an opposite course. It is an outgoing force engaged almost exclusively in gathering as many experiences as possible in life. It is an aggressive and active vibration responsible for expansion and progress, with variety and experience as its chief characteristics. It is also the vibration of the senses and its subjects possess the capacity to motivate with equal dexterity on the physical, emotional and mental planes of life. The intuitive faculty is also keen. These faculties are illustrated by the 5's middle position among the 9 digits, four before and four after, and its centre position in the numerological grid, which makes it the only number that has communication with all others.

Five personalities are not easy to analyse or classify into a particular type, for their restlessness, changeability and versatility are bewildering. Their mercurial nature is the result of the influence of the planet Mercury. Some other traits include flamboyance, speed, energy, wit, skill in repartee, enthusiasm, impulsiveness, adaptability, sociability, resourcefulness, wanderlust, alertness, drive, competitiveness, intelligence, volatility and personal magnetism. Curiosity and readiness to plunge into new ventures are other notable features. Their resourcefulness and ability to make instant decisions help them to overcome any temporary difficulty they may encounter as a result of sudden action. To the average Five personality, life is a permanent question mark.

More general attributes of the vibration are bohemianism and unconventionality. Total absence of oral frustration makes them great talkers. They have an unusual ability to influence and motivate others through the medium of speech, for they speak with conviction, though not necessarily with depth of knowledge. When aroused they use their power of speech to criticise and hurt. While Three personalities enjoy quality of speech, the Fives possess power of speech for their delivery is accompanied by emotional expression as well as personal magnetism. Due to their vibrant nature, they find themselves constantly in the limelight.

A quick turnover in relationships may be the fate of most Fives as a result of their desire to keep moving on. Close friendships are rarely maintained, unless it is expedient to do so.

They have no affinity with a particular number or numbers but are able to get along with all types of people. However, they will not hesitate to reject anyone who is unable to keep up with their agile minds and high-powered activity. They are highly strung personalities and are so alert and quick to react that they have no understanding and tolerance of slow thinking and slow moving people. As this is a high tension vibration most Fives are inclined to live on their nerves, experiencing many highs and lows in temperament. Owing to frequent outbursts of energy they suffer from bouts of exhaustion, but bounce back to normal after short periods of rest. They also recover quickly after indulging in physical excesses.

They are totally extroverted types, but their type of extroversion is focused more on activity and movement than social intercourse. While their personal lives may be disorganised, most of them will try to run and organise the lives of others. They make their own plans and expect others to fall in with them. Governed by the vibration of progress and growth, they are always looking ahead and are found in the forefront of any onward movement. These people have an innate understanding of the need for change, realising that opportunities for progress are found through new and changing circumstances. More major changes take place in their lives than in the lives of people governed by other vibrations.

Some desirable qualities lacking in the average Five personality — unless helped by other numbers — are dependability in routine duties, constancy, tolerance of slower personalities, self-control and the ability to relax.

Negative Fives are subject to extreme restlessness, uncontrolled activity, a constant desire for change, severe tension, deceit and extravagance. They can be irresponsible, untruthful, argumentative, self-indulgent, unstable and tend to abuse freedom. They are cagey and shifty and are regarded as untrustworthy by cautious people.

Five personalities live for the present and spend money freely. They will not question the price of an article or spend time looking for a bargain. They are fond of speculation and gambling and will not avoid a challenge of any sort or fail to take advantage of a "get rich" scheme that may come their way. Those strongly influenced by this vibration enjoy a good measure of success in games of chance.

As workers, they are intelligent, energetic and able to handle more than one task at a time but they become unsettled in subordinate positions if their freedom of movement is

restricted. They are at their best when on the move and in contact with people and when there is some degree of risk and
danger in their undertakings. Confinement and routine duties
quickly stifle their well-being. The best salespersons and front
people are produced by this vibration, and they also do well in
travel and communication. They make good executives and
have the ability to stimulate others and keep them constantly
alert and enthusiastic. Fives who take to the legal profession
will develop expertise in advocacy. They are not given to research
work or in-depth studies on account of the urge to move on, and
as a result they gather a variety of knowledge but rarely find
time to specialise.

People with Five personalities radiate a sensuous charm
with a strong attraction to the opposite sex — an attraction that
could extend to several people at the same time. They are more
allured by the sensual side of life than those influenced by other
vibrations. Their urge for variety in sexual expression places
considerable stress upon themselves and their loved ones, who
often have to bear with competition. Many of these people will
hesitate to marry for fear of surrendering their freedom. On the
other hand, many young Fives make hasty and eventually un-
successful marriages as a result of their impulsiveness, desire
for experience and impulsion to move out of the family home.
The Fives' need for personal freedom is very strong and their
partners in any close relationship should make few demands
and be free from jealousy and possessiveness, for attempts to
restrict or reform them will rarely be successful. They will soon
end a partnership that has become dull, restricting and demanding. Their partners will need to assume domestic responsibility as this vibration is decidedly not a home-oriented one.
Tolerance, understanding and trust will bring out the loyalty of
the Five.

Children strongly influenced by this vibration will be
physically and emotionally active from an early age. Hyperactivity and tension will be problems with the more negative ones.
Their curiosity to explore and experience the world about them
will also be displayed early. This strong trait of the 5 vibration,
as well as its impulsiveness, will make many of its younger subjects accident prone and inclined to a variety of other adventuresome and mischievous actions. They should be trained to
look before they leap. They are intelligent, observant and extremely alert children and are instantly aware of whatever is
going on around them. They are strongly competitive and exhibit
considerable physical courage when exposed to a challenge or

danger. Because of their quick reflexes they make good acrobats though this could make them somewhat reckless and inclined to take unnecessary risks. They usually excel in all sports, especially those where very fast movement is required.

Restlessness will be the major problem. Five children will insist on being heard. Their need for freedom of speech and action will be observed at an early age. Strict control of their education is needed to contain their natural aptitude in many directions and their tendency to seek experience in several ways. If not, they will be inclined to switch courses of study too frequently. While the best all-rounders are produced by this vibration, the "Jack of all trades and master of none" is also frequently found here. At home they can be irresponsible, especially with chores and timetables.

The best days for Five personalities to transact business are Wednesdays and Fridays, especially if they fall on a Five day, such as the 5th, 14th and 23rd. They are leaders in fashion and their versatility is also reflected in their attire, which often is not only up-to-date but well in advance of current trends. They take particular care of their hands and fingers and show a great aversion to plunging their hands into dirt of any sort. Their best colours are white, light greys, yellows and all bright and glistening colours. Their jewel is the diamond set in silver or platinum.

While the 5th day of any month produces the straightforward Five personalities, the 14th and 23rd form the complex ones. Those born on the 14th are self-assured and physically oriented and those born on the 23rd are artistic and movement loving. People born on the 15th and 25th, though not Five personalities, are strongly influenced by this number.

VIBRATION NUMBER 6
Letters F, O, X

Following immediately after the 5 stage of freedom, wanderlust and experience, the 6 vibration brings into operation an energy of a mental nature, having a tranquil and stable effect upon those subject to it. Harmony and balance are its noted features as a result of an equal interaction of physical and spiritual elements. Under these influences, Six personalities seek comfort of the body as well as serenity of mind.

This is a receptive vibration ruled by the planet Venus, and people under its influence are extroverted types with evenly balanced personal traits and a loving nature. Their love of home and their attachment to everything associated with the home and family set them apart from subjects of other vibrations. The homing call of this vibration is so strong that it is regarded as the vibration of domesticity. Home entertainment is brought to a fine art by all Sixes. On the other hand, they are strictly short-term visitors for their need to return home soon takes hold of them. As guests they will not be found overstaying their welcome.

Positive Sixes are responsible, harmonious, congenial, sympathetic, tactful, understanding, just, conscientious, peaceful, unselfish, diplomatic, dutiful, loyal, humanitarian and hospitable. They are also recognised by their conservative habits, logical thinking and analytical minds. These Sixes cannot be hurried or pushed into making a decision as action is taken only after much deliberation. Haste and impulse are characteristics not found in these subjects.

All Sixes are group-centred, idealistic and comprehensive in their outlook. A high sense of civic duty gives them the energy to maintain a stable and happy home, as well as engage in a variety of social responsibilities, particularly in areas of community welfare. They find it easier than others to bridge the generation gap and communicate without effort with young and old alike. They project a parental image and the personal warmth they unconsciously radiate attracts people of all ages. Without intent or design, they frequently find themselves acting as counsellors, teachers, guides, healers and instructors, and derive a great deal of pleasure in doing so.

They are pleasant conversationalists and excellent story-tellers. It is easy to enter into an argument with these people as their logical and analytical minds urge them to question any statement that is not factual. However, they are always fair and good humoured in presenting their points of view. Good food, taken in refined company and elegant surroundings, the fine arts, home entertainment and simple family life are other pursuits they enjoy. Their love of comfort and ease often exceeds their capacity to take adequate physical exercise. When this characteristic is combined with their love of good food and drink, excess weight may be a problem, especially if a 4 vibration also influences the personality. A great deal of organisation and planning is brought into their personal and business lives. Domestic discord, dishonesty, vulgarity, speed and loneliness are most upsetting to their well-being.

Some qualities not strongly present in the average Six personality are a competitive spirit, instant action and reaction, ambition, self-assertiveness and self-discipline.

Negative Six personalities are subject to worry, moodiness and depression. They are overanxious about affairs of the home and could be nagging and meddlesome. They have fixed minds and dogmatic opinions. They can also be escapists from responsibility, unsympathetic, abnormally jealous, domestic tyrants, preoccupied with self, fearful and intolerant.

In business and home management, caution is shown in money matters and they are very security conscious. They are neither impulsive spenders nor gamblers or speculators. They place their money only in safe investments. They will always manage to balance their budget, but they are inclined to worry unnecessarily about their financial future.

Good Six personalities excel in positions of responsibility and trust. They are congenial workers and soon earn the respect of their colleagues. This vibration produces, among others, teachers, counsellors, social workers, cooks and business people dealing in home products, food and accommodation. They are not ruthless or strongly competitive in business. The 6 is also a healing vibration and its subjects are attracted to all areas of healing associated with the body and mind. Many excel in community and humanitarian activities.

Love rules these people and the giving and receiving of love is their paramount purpose in life. They are, nevertheless, not as physically passionate as subjects of some other numbers, nor are they very demonstrative. Controlled by a mental vibration, reason overshadows their thoughts and actions. Loyalty and devotion to their families are the means by which they display their great capacity for love. Rarely do these people remain single as the basic need for companionship and homemaking takes priority over other considerations. Some Sixes, however, remain single if faced with the responsibility of a dependent parent or close relative. They are still driven by the need to establish a true home setting, irrespective of whether it is maintained for the benefit of dependants or a partner and children.

Loyalty to their partners is natural. They will not jeopardise the comforts and dignity of home life by indulging in clandestine affairs. Most Sixes make successful marriages. They have a natural flair to choose the right partners and work towards the success of the partnership. However, in some instances, the decision to marry and the choice of a partner is the one occasion where deliberation may give way to haste. Their fundamental need for companionship and a home of their own may override their natural caution. They are responsible parents and guardians and willingly accept full responsibility for the upbringing of their children. They could however be possessive and overprotective of their loved ones, often blind to their faults and inclined to smother them with attention.

Attachment to home is the distinguishing feature of all Six children. They will carry out their share, and more, of domestic chores willingly and without effort. They display an early fondness for cooking. They are not sentimental and cuddly types, though they need and will in turn return a great deal of love and affection. Domestic harmony is as essential to these Six children as it is to their Two counterparts, though they will recover more quickly than the Twos from upheavals in the home and will assume any added responsibility if required to do so.

They are highly intelligent children who are not aggressive, egoistic or boastful and who accept personal achievement as a matter of course. They should not be pushed into competition but allowed to choose their own avenues of study and sport. They set their own pace and will retreat within themselves if pressured into action. Gentle persuasion and guidance will always succeed. The logical thinking of this vibration operates from a very early age. A Six child will not be persuaded by arguments not based on reason. Parents could avoid conflict by substituting emotional arguments with thoughtful and reasonable ones.

The best days for these personalities to transact business are Tuesdays, Thursdays and Fridays, especially if they fall on the 6th, 15th or 24th day of any month.

The average Six personality is not fashion-conscious and their style and choice of clothing is for comfort and durability. The colours they should use are blue, pink, rose and orange. Their stones are the emerald, turquoise and opal, set in gold.

Sixes born on the 24th have many similarities to the straightforward Sixes born on the 6th but possess wider scope for motivation on the emotional and physical planes as well as the mental plane. Those born on the 15th day could be difficult to recognise as true Sixes owing to the influence of two aggressive and adventuresome vibrations in the forefront of their personalities. Essential 6 qualities, however, remain firm in the background.

VIBRATION NUMBER 7
Letters G, P, Y

The state of equilibrium between the physical and spiritual forces maintained in the 6 vibration no longer prevails in the 7, for now the spiritual forces outweigh those of the physical.

Known as the number of God, the 7 is the symbol of a vibration representing the mystic element in life. It has few qualities in common with other numbers and stands apart with many unique features of its own. The influence of the mysterious planet Neptune — the planet of Divinity — is seen here.

People influenced by this vibration, not surprisingly, are detached and aloof in their manner with a keen attraction towards contemplative and meditative pleasures. Their natural inclination is to look into the soul of things, to question the unexplained, to engage in the abstract and attempt to discover the cause of things rather than be satisfied with the effects. While most others are prepared to accept without question various concepts and dogmas put forward by spiritual thinkers, the Sevens need to gain knowledge independently and seek their own spiritual unfolding. In order to do so, they seek solitude and silence.

Sustained sociability in these persons cannot be taken for granted; social involvement and popularity rate a low priority in their scheme of things. They are strongly individual- istic and are the true loners, at perfect ease in their own com- pany. This attitude, unfortunately, makes others feel isolated in the company of strong Sevens. They are often misunderstood until others realise that they are, in fact, not unsocial but that their need for their own company is greater than their need for the company of others. When the occasions arise they are able to enjoy company and yet maintain their detached attitude. They rarely step beyond person-to-person communication. Loved ones apart, this non-dependence on others for their happiness is a source of considerable power to these people.

Irrespective of their station in life, strong Sevens possess poise, personal dignity and a certain mystery in their manner. The eyes of all strong Sevens project a deep and distant expres- sion. They are not loudspoken or demanding in their manner but have a quiet way of expressing themselves. They speak only when they have something worthwhile to say and specialised knowledge is usually shown, along with an unusual ability to reduce complex matters to a few precise words, pregnant with meaning. This talent is often used to deflate the opinions of pom- pous people. An instant aversion is shown towards frivolous and casual conversation.

The constant pursuit of worthwhile knowledge distin- guishes them from all other personalities. They are self-teachers and often take to specialisation in a particular field of knowl- edge. While subjects of other vibrations may pursue and acquire power by means of wealth and position, the Sevens accomplish this through learning, for knowledge to them is synonymous with power. In turn, they give their admiration and respect only to those they recognise as being intellectually and spiritually advanced.

Other distinguishing features of the average Seven are a striving for perfection and a need to analyse all aspects of life, for nothing is accepted by them at face value. Issues that engross the attention of the average person will leave these Sevens totally disinterested. Their thoughts are generally focused away from mundane issues. Melancholy and frustration may often result from clashes between their yearning to live on a higher plane and the practical responsibilities of life. While engaged in this personal battle their reactions to the ways of others may not always be favourable. Their mental courage far exceeds their physical courage as they realise that there is a world to be discovered with greater fascination and rewards than anything the commercial and social worlds have to offer.

Most Sevens have an aura of unapproachability, which is another reason why they are misunderstood by others. Their love of privacy, even secrecy, and unwillingness to explain themselves contribute to this impression. More loners, celibates and stoics come from this vibration than from any other. True nature lovers, who easily tune in with natural surroundings, are also found here. It will be most unusual to find a Seven personality who is not a keen gardener and environmentalist. They also have a strong attraction towards old things and frequently turn to the study of ancient history, archaeology, palaeontology, anthropology, ancient architecture and ancient music. They like to visit museums, archives, old homes and gardens and are attracted to businesses dealing with anti-quarian objects.

Some desirable qualities not found in the average Seven are adaptability, optimism, emotional expression, tolerance, self-appreciation, fluent oral expression and spontaneity. There is certainly a need for them to loosen up a bit. Unhappiness is sometimes experienced through their reluctance to let themselves go, and from their habit of being too critical and suspicious of others.

The urge to run away from life's responsibilities is the main problem with negative Sevens. They are totally intro-verted and generally unhappy people who seek various forms of escapism, often through alcohol. They exhibit negative traits such as stubbornness, impracticality, rebellion, abnormal suspicion of the motives of others, melancholy, sarcasm, deceit and intolerance. They are generally cold personalities. Lack of trust in themselves followed by distrust of others deters them from entering into emotional relationships. Great difficulty will be experienced in reaching them and attempting to help them overcome their many self-imposed limitations.

All Sevens have an unusual money sense and are able to develop considerable expertise in handling and investing money. They are not gamblers or speculators but rely largely on specialised knowledge and intuition. Emotion and impulse are not brought into their financial dealings. Their philosophical attitudes also keep them unattached to and independent of their wealth and other material possessions.

Seven personalities work best alone. They make excellent research workers and should avoid team work and equal partnerships. They need to be free to make their own decisions and could also be quite intolerant of people who do not measure up to their high standards of duty and efficiency. While some of them will be bankers, investors and teachers at tertiary levels, others will be in forestry, agriculture, farming, water conservation and anything to do with nature and the land. Still another group may take to science and technology.

As marriage partners and parents they tend to be possessive. They are loyal, protective and good providers. All major decisions within the family are made by them. Marriage is successful when based on mental, cultural and spiritual compatibility. Though emotionally undemonstrative and embarrassed by sentiment, their love is very deep and constant. A real effort is made by them to preserve the privacy and sanctity of family life.

Being self-sufficient people, they dislike being fussed over and bothered with details. Talkative and society-loving partners are certain to cause problems. The personal magnetism of these people is known and appreciated only by family members and a few close friends. They are romantic only in the right setting. No personality can turn off as quickly as a Seven if the atmosphere is not conducive to lovemaking.

Seven children stand out in any family or group on account of their fundamental qualities of detachment and aloofness. A seriousness beyond their years is noticeable. They will show a tendency to avoid group participation and will pass through their school days forming no more than one or two close friendships. Great distress will be shown if they are forced into a central position in extracurricular activities.

They have exceptionally probing minds and are anxious to investigate the nature of things. They have an inclination towards science, technology and the natural sciences. They are mentally active and do not take kindly to being taught by others; they prefer to be left alone to observe and draw their own conclusions. Parents and guardians must respect these children's need for privacy, for their best development takes place in concentration, contemplation and seclusion.

A sense of loneliness is felt by them in their tender years as a result of hesitation in company, but they are soon able to find companionship and contentment within themselves. Once this discovery is made they blossom into strong, self-confident children and their greatest strength will be this newly dis-covered self-sufficiency. Corporal punishment will be worthless on these thinkers. If the subtle mental approach is not used, they will simply withdraw within themselves. They will be good at most sports though not strongly competitive. Winning or losing will be taken with the innate philosophical attitude of the 7 vibration.

The best days for Seven personalities to transact busi-ness are Sundays and Mondays, especially if they fall on the 7th, 16th or 25th day of any month. They are conservative in dress and should avoid dark colours. Green, white, yellow and all light shades are best suited. Their stones are pearls, moonstones and onyx set in silver.

Concentrated 7 characteristics are only found in those born on the 7th day. The sociability of the 6 vibration and ambi-tion of the 1 obscure many of the recluse tendencies of the 7 in those born on the 16th. People born on the 25th are not easily recognised as Sevens. Outwardly they may appear extroverted owing to their love of movement but many strong 7 qualities remain firm in the background. This latter group certainly possess greater scope for variety of expression than those born on the 7th who are content with intensity of expression. The 17th day and the 27th day also produce personalities powerfully influenced by the 7 vibration. These people may display more 7 characteristics than those born on the 16th and 25th.

VIBRATION NUMBER 8
Letters H, Q, Z

Whereas the 7 vibration represents, by and large, the inner realms of mental enquiry, the 8 vibration takes an opposite direction and stands for intense activity in the outer regions of worldly affairs. This is the last single vibration or number expressing individual characteristics. The 9 vibration which follows represents a combination of the attributes of all previous vibrations. The 8 vibration is an embodiment of power directed into business, commerce, organisations, administration and executive authority. At the same time, a deep-seated spirituality is manifested in the form of incorruptibility, responsibility, honour, justice and philanthrophy. The double strength of the 4 vibration and many qualities of the 1 vibration combine here to operate on a much higher frequency, forming high-minded personalities with greatly widened perspectives of life. The single-minded thrust of the ambitions of the 1 vibration is now tempered by judgement, foresight, justice and considerable practical knowledge.

The 8 vibration is known as the number of success for the power it gives its subjects for advancement, achievement and production. The thought processes of Eight personalities are channelled along constructive lines with constant awareness and concern for future needs.

The positive side of this vibration also provides sound commonsense, deliberation, arbitration, tact, authority, leadership, tenacity, self-assertiveness, self-reliance, strength of purpose and unlimited ambition.

Active and receptive qualities play an even role in this vibration, although, as an even number, it is placed among the receptive vibrations. Those subject to it are also extroverted, friendly and understanding, with sensitivity for the problems of others. Their emotionalism makes them vulnerable to criticism, interference and the callous remarks of others. However, they have a fine knack of concealing this vulnerability behind a facade of inscrutability.

In personal relationships they are tactful and gentle and at the same time firm and authoritative if necessary. They can be identified from a habit of unconsciously directing and managing people around them. Usually direct and matter-of-fact in speech, they are not found among the great talkers. As public speakers, they exude power rather than artistry. They are conservative in all their ways and live strictly within the established order of society. No free thinkers or bohemians are found with this number predominating. Many eminent professional sportsmen, sportswomen and coaches are found here. They are courageous, determined and enduring competitors.

Qualities not found in the average Eight personality are artistic imagination, devotion to private study, ability to relax, a ready sense of humour and humility.

Common traits found on the negative side include

irritability, restlessness, aggressiveness, despair, fear, excess of materialism, intolerance, callousness and an abnormal desire for personal recognition.

All Eights have an excellent money sense and are un-equalled in financial management of businesses or non-commercial enterprises. The best business minds, organisers and executives with a fine knack for delegation of work are produced by this number. This faculty for choosing the right people for the right tasks is one of the secrets of success of these personalities. They do have a strong tendency to become totally involved in their work, into which they put a great deal of emotional effort. Heart and mind are used with equal force, thus risking much emotional strain. The need for relaxation in areas other than regular work is often overlooked. Impulsive action is alien to those of this vibration. Considerable deliberation and planning takes place before any moves are made. Impartiality is another admirable quality seen in these people, and judgements handed down by them on any matter are usually unquestionable.

These personalities soon find themselves in positions of authority and make splendid superiors. On the one hand, they are hard taskmasters who suffer frequent frustration when subordinates do not measure up to their standards of efficiency and on the other hand they do not hesitate to show their appreciation for high-quality performance. Their own dedication and enthusiasm make them leaders by example before any other means need to be adopted. Restrictions should not be placed on their ambitions as all Eights possess the potential to rise well above the average in professional or business fields.

As in the case of Four personalities, reliance is not placed on luck or assistance from others but on steady, hard work. The accumulation of wealth is associated with the acquisition of power, and this is what all Eights really aspire to. Those who have succeeded in achieving this goal, however, do not find real fulfilment unless a balance is maintained — on the one hand between power and material possessions and on the other hand between ethical, moral and spiritual values. Their inner spirituality cannot be overlooked since this forms the bedrock of the 8 vibration. Enslavement to power at the expense of personal peace, contentment and humility often allows room for pride to take over the personality and this detracts from the pleasure of their success.

Partners in marriage, or any personal relationship, give more of their labour and affection than they receive, for these Eight personalities tend to involve themselves in the business side of their lives at the expense of home, loved ones and social responsibilities. Their partners need to prod them into meeting their social obligations. Their homes are seldom open for entertainment and, if given their own way, will be kept strictly as a family preserve. Their apparent unsociability is unintentional and is due to their intense dedication to their businesses or professions. They need the precious little time they allow themselves for enjoyment of their families.

Eights are excellent providers who take great pride in their families. They are also very loving and greatly in need of love but all too frequently do not find time for romance, sentiment and personal involvement with family affairs. The authority they are accustomed to in public life is too often exercised in the domestic scene.

The feelings of Eight children are easily hurt, until emotion is brought under control with maturity. Their behaviour is often tinged with aggression, for they will take some time to understand the power that lies within them. This aggression will be exhibited to a greater degree if there is also a strong 1 vibration in the birth date.

Their capacity to take control and assume the role of leader will be revealed early, especially if an emergency arises. Their innate sense of justice makes them strong supporters of the underdog. Some friction is bound to follow when they meet up with other Eight personalities. While being encouraged to participate in all kinds of sport, their education should be carried to tertiary levels, for these children are not meant to occupy subordinate and unskilled positions in life. Subjects chosen for study should be those that will lead them into business, administration and the law. High ambition should be encouraged. They are serious-minded children due to the lack of sparkle, quick wit and imagination of the 8 vibration. This is not a domesticated number and Eight children may not willingly participate in their share of home duties, but will be found to be neat and orderly in their personal habits.

The best days for Eights to transact business are Saturdays, Sundays and Mondays, especially if they fall on the 8th, 17th and 26th day of any month.

Eight personalities choose clothing of the best quality and they pay careful attention to detail. Their best colours are dark grey, black, dark blue, purple and brown. Light shades should be avoided. The precious stones they should wear are the amethyst, black pearl, black diamond, lapis lazuli and other dark coloured stones.

The strongest Eight personalities are those born on the 8th day of any month, while the 17th and 26th produce Eight personalities with qualified characteristics. Those born on the 17th should take to banking and investment, while those born on the 26th should succeed in businesses relating to accommodation and home products. The 8 vibration has a powerful influence over those born on the 18th and 28th and needs to be taken into serious consideration when these birth dates are examined.

VIBRATION NUMBER 9
Letters I and R

As the highest of all primary or single-digit numbers, the 9 symbolises a vibration as powerful as the 8 but without direct relation to the business world. It is known principally as the vibration of wisdom and stands for a high state of mental and spiritual advancement. It is, in fact, an all-embracing vibration signifying completion. It contains the initiative of the 1, the gentleness and grace of the 2, the imagination and self-expression of the 3, the sense of proportion of the 4, the alertness and progress of the 5, the responsibility of the 6, the desire for perfection of the 7, the judgement of the 8 and, as a natural progression, the wisdom, compassion and universality of its own.

Some unique features of this number may be seen mathematically in the 360 degree circle, indicating completeness: $3 + 6 + 0 = 9$. Also, when all single digits from 1 to 9 are added up: $1 + 2 + 3 + 4 + 5 + 6 + 7 + 8 + 9 = 45 = 9$. Further, when any number is multiplied by 9, for example $8 \times 9 = 72 = 9$, the answer always adds up to 9. When 9 is added to 9: $9 + 9 = 18 = 9$, it reproduces itself. On the other hand, whenever 9 is added to any number the result is always that number, for example $9 + 5 = 14 = 5$, or $9 + 8 = 17 = 8$.

As a far-reaching and impersonal vibration the 9 does not confine its subjects to self, family, community or country. While the 1 vibration holds its subjects to self and self-advancement, the 9, at the opposite end of the single-digit spectrum, leads them out of all confinement into consciousness of humanity at large, irrespective of race, religion, geographical and traditional divisions. The 1 gives individuality, the 9 universality.

Well-established Nine personalities are selfless and broad-minded humanitarians. Whenever circumstances permit, they lead a cosmopolitan lifestyle and invariably maintain a cosmopolitan outlook. Other distinguishing features of these people are understanding, forgiveness, honour, honesty, charm, generosity, idealism, personal magnetism, intuition, extrasensory perception and great sensitivity to atmosphere, colour and sound. They also have spiritual and psychic gifts, including that of intuition, which can offer them revelationary knowledge, which is not based on strict logic and gives them insights into identifying mental or physical illness. They share the love of meditative pleasures and enquiry into the mystical side of life with Seven personalities, but unlike the retiring Sevens who tend to keep their knowledge to themselves, the Nines spread their wisdom around and make every endeavour to give practical expression to their ideals. All their actions are influenced by their high ideals, spiritual values and generosity.

They travel because of their wide interests in human culture. They soon gather a great deal of knowledge, particularly in the fine arts. The cultural aspects of life become as important to the developed Nines as the spiritual and humanitarian sides. Many strong Nines, however, often run the risk of gathering a considerable store of learning and in the meantime losing touch with its practical application.

This vibration attracts more power and fame to its subjects than the 8 or any other vibration could ever hope to achieve. Their global outlook, humanitarianism and wisdom give them a degree of superiority far greater than others. Their remarkable restorative powers are also shown by their capacity to re-establish their lives after adversity or upheaval.

Many younger Nines may suffer from self-centredness until they outgrow self-love and turn from the habit of receiving to the practice of giving. The true nature of the 9 vibration will manifest itself, and much personal frustration and unhappiness will be overcome, as soon as a selfless attitude is developed. The greatest danger faced by Nines is selfishness and the greatest challenge is surmounting the obstacle of self-love.

Some traits that tend to inhibit the potential of many Nines are indecision, procrastination, lack of concentration, impracticality, lack of commercial sense and impressionability. They keep emotional grudges to themselves until they become overwhelming and explode in virulent, critical outbursts. The depth of wisdom in this vibration places great pressure on them to control their emotions whenever they meet with narrowness, bigotry and parochialism in people who do not possess the same breadth of vision. The stronger ones are able to contain themselves and even express compassion. The weaker ones often lose control of themselves and resort to outbursts of anger and biting sarcasm.

The problems associated with negative Nines are a general feeling of bitterness towards the world and ill-temper. Their abnormal fear of having their feelings hurt makes them either defensive or aggressive; they are intolerant of opinions with which they disagree and have fanatical religious beliefs and unstable emotions. They can also be egocentric, dictatorial, extremely secretive, uncooperative, and indulge in aimless dreaming. They spend most of their time criticising other people and their most unfortunate problem is that they want to be loved but are not prepared to give their love in return. A negative Nine entering a family by marriage is certain to cause problems at all family gatherings.

Generosity, for which Nine personalities are noted, is displayed in the handling of their finances. The average Nine is regarded as a 'soft touch'. The basic compassion of the 9 vibration combined with impressionability and indifference towards accumulation of material wealth contribute to this situation.

These personalities function best as professionals. They lack business acumen because of their generosity and disinterest in commercial competition. They are best suited to a wide contact with all types of people, especially in areas where the 9 quality of human understanding can be used. If these personalities happen to be involved in mundane work that inhibits their imagination and resources, it is advisable that they find hobbies in the fields of art and literature as outlets for their cultural talents. Many Nines who are not able to reach the full extent of their potential in their professions find satisfactory personal outlets in charitable works, involvement in relief, welfare and refugee organisations, or similar humanitarian activity within the established churches.

As marriage partners positive Nines are broad-minded, sympathetic, tolerant and free in giving. Their spouses, unless of a similar bent, may often find it hard to cope with their generosity and breadth of vision. Problems are bound to arise with narrow-minded and materialistic partners. Nines are usually attracted to people who measure up to their standards of idealism and refinement. They are passionate and devoted with the right partners and always give more than they receive. They are not domesticated, however, and personal freedom is needed for their many outside activities.

Most precocious children are Nine personalities. Their

opinions frequently have their elders amazed and wondering how and where such knowledge was acquired. The innate wisdom of the 9 vibration reveals itself as soon as these children are able to communicate in speech. They are superior children who, with proper care and guidance, will grow into superior adults. From an early age they should be guided away from self-centredness, narrow-mindedness and extreme forms of nationalism. Their early conflict between selfishness and the establishment of an unselfish lifestyle will become evident by sudden changes in moods from tolerance and extreme generosity to coldness, withdrawal and self-interest. They are liable to change swiftly from a state of great happiness to one of anger and disillusionment. They are deeply emotional but unable to demonstrate their emotions except in sudden outbursts of temper when their minds can no longer contain conflicting sentiments. Much joy is found by them in contemplative and meditative pleasures. As refined, courteous and non-aggressive children, they will not be fierce competitors. This will not hinder them since their intelligence and natural talent in many directions will usually see them out as winners.

The best days for Nine personalities to transact business of any sort are Tuesdays, Thursdays and Fridays, especially if these days fall on the 9th, 18th or 27th day of any month.

An international touch is seen in their choice of clothes. Colours that suit them best are red, carmine, lavender, olive, pink, wine and rose. They should avoid black. Their stones are the ruby, garnet, bloodstones and other red coloured stones.

While unqualified Nine personalities are found among those born on the 9th day of any month, those born on the 18th day are disguised by the strength of the businesslike 1 and 8 vibrations. These people are capable of considerable achievement since they are backed by the internationalism of the underlying 9. The 27th also produces outstanding Nines with a greater leaning towards non-competitive pursuits and the study of the inner side of life.

THE MASTER VIBRATIONS
Numbers 11 and 22

Beyond the 9 vibration there are two others of much higher frequency symbolised by the unreduced numbers 11 and 22. Known as Master numbers, they may be found in any of the six Spheres of Influence and will have control of the personality according to the nature of the particular Sphere of Influence in which they are found. These are intense and powerful vibrations and the majority of people who possess them find it difficult to live continously within their high frequencies. Only a few advanced individuals are able to remain permanently on these high vibratory levels. When not living up to the demands of these Master vibrations, these people revert to the influence of the base numbers 2 and 4 respectively.

When these numbers are found it is best to interpret them, in the first instance, as two 1's reducing to a 2, and two 2's reducing to a 4. After close examination of the overall chart we may consider to what extent the qualities of the unreduced Master numbers influence the personality.

VIBRATION NUMBER 11

The 11 vibration is a higher frequency than the 9, which itself is the highest of the single-digit vibrations. The 11 shares many characteristics with the 9, particularly the surrender of personal ambition for spiritual and cultural interests. It is essentially the vibration of spirit and those influenced by it are non-worldly and non-commercial in outlook. Being an intensified vibration it makes great demands upon the personality, especially if it is found in the sphere of destiny. The two 1s of the 11 contribute positivity and willpower, adding considerable strength to the underlying 2, which is not found in the straightforward 2 vibration.

The outstanding features of this vibration are inspiration, vision, intuition, spirituality, evangelism, zeal and a gift of prophecy and revelation. Individuals living up to the full strength of this Master number become powerful orators, evangelists, missionaries, reformers and philosophers. The average Eleven personality finds it hard to resist the urge to expound firm opinions to all and sundry.

These people also take to science and excel in space age scientific inventions. They possess to a greater degree the inventive genius of the plain One personalities. Their inventions, however, are not confined to scientific interests but could range from designing clothes to domestic products and a whole range of activity for improving living conditions. Idealism rather than commercialism is behind the Elevens' urge to invent. They are also found as psychologists, astronomers, astrologers and mediums. Their keenness to explore the inner being is assisted by strong intuition and psychic ability. Their need for artistic expression is equally strong.

Another extraordinary characteristic of these people is a constant desire to improve and reform, especially in the social and spiritual realms of life. They live in a world of their own ideas, ideals and visions, often failing to understand and tolerate others who cannot share their elevated thoughts. In turn, they are frequently misunderstood and subjected to ridicule by more earth-bound people. Though not leaders of people in the usual sense, they are leaders in ideas, concepts and new schemes for human welfare. They are always ahead of times and are considered the forerunners of the new Aquarian age.

Most Elevens need to be more practical. Too often they become infatuated with their own ideals and lose touch with mundane issues and human relationships. Due to their non-materialistic outlook, they have little desire to hold on to their possessions and are therefore spontaneous givers. They would rather give than receive. As they are motivated by the vibration of spirit they are able to drive themselves to greater lengths than most others, and as the spirit never tires they do not consider retirement from their activities.

Master numbers, too, have their negative sides and those peculiar to the 11 are dogmatism, fanaticism, superiority, impracticability, indecision, aimlessness and eccentricity. They are also well known as people who do not always practise what they preach.

As partners in marriage they are not easy to cope with unless their spouses are on the same wavelength. Their advanced ideas and unconventional lifestyle sometimes place a strain on the domestic scene. Their partners should not be materialistic or parochial in their desires and attitudes. The Elevens will not show patience, tolerance or understanding if there is incompatibility in a partnership. Many Elevens tend to lose personal direction, bringing disorder into their lives and the lives of those close to them.

For special days, dress, colours and stones, those of the 2 vibration apply.

Only two types of Elevens are found in the First Sphere of Influence. The straightforward ones born on the 11th and the complex personalities born on the 29th. A great deal of emotion takes control of those born on the 29th.

VIBRATION NUMBER 22

While the 11 vibration brings out the spiritual messenger, the 22 produces the spiritual builder, combining both spirit and matter. The vibratory power of the 11 is doubled in the 22, giving it not only greater intensity in the spiritual realms but also the balancing gift of practicality. It contains the attributes of every other vibration in a well-balanced combination of the spiritual and practical. This combination gives the 22 a consolidated power not found in any of the other numbers.

The 22 vibration may appear in any of the six Spheres of Influence but will be most influential in the first and second, as the personality type or as destiny. Positive Twenty-twos are found only when the number 1 is present in the birth date, such as 22 . 1 . 1966 or 10 . 12 . 1935 = 22. A generally negative birth date will be 22 . 5 . 1958 = 32 = 5. A badly negative birth date will be 22 . 2 . 1924 = 22. The willpower of the 1 vibration is needed in order to handle this Master vibration.

The practicality of the basic 4 of this Master vibration works in harmony with the spirituality of the 22, making its subjects practical visionaries and practical idealists operating on a horizon that is wider and more comprehensive than the 9 or the 11. While sharing the same international outlook as the Nines and Elevens, the Twenty-twos have the potential to fulfil their ideas, dreams, visions and projects.

An advanced academic education will be of great advantage to these individuals so that there will be no outside hindrance to their using the unlimited potential they possess. They are mature souls who gather knowledge speedily, with the complementary urge to put this knowledge into practical use. They are well balanced emotionally, though they sometimes have difficulty coming to terms with their higher spiritual nature and the many practical responsibilities in the material aspects of their lives. This conflict is overcome once they develop a sense of objectivity and no longer associate their personal feelings with the many activities in which they become involved. The lifestyle of these people is unconventional and some opposition from the establishment can be expected when they begin to act in terms of their own potential or build upon the blueprints put forward by the Eleven messengers. They are generally late starters in life since a considerable amount of searching is done before they make a definite start. Thereafter there is no holding them back.

Totally negative Twenty-twos are the opposite of their positive counterparts. Personal gain is the governing influence in their lives. They are materialistic and are obsessed with accumulating wealth and power. They are also lonely and self-centred people with strong inferiority complexes. They could be ruthless in their bid for power. The global outlook remains and much fraud and crime on an international scale is a temptation to these people.

Twenty-twos, whether positive or negative, cannot be tied down to domesticity. However, their capacity to play a dual role as good providers and protectors of home and family as well as being public figures is soon recognised by their partners. They will demand freedom and resent interference, dominance and any restrictions on their movements.

Their special days for business activity, dress, colours and stones are the same as those for the 4 vibration.

Only one Twenty-two personality type appears in the First Sphere of Influence, namely those born on the 22nd day of any month.

THE CIPHER *0*

While the zero does not represent special characteristics it does serve to intensify the features of a number to which it is attached and, in turn, the personality as a whole. It may have the effect of reinforcing the positive or negative aspects of a person. The position of the zero in the birth date has to be taken into consideration when determining the extent of its effect on the personality. It could be in a position with no appreciable influence on the personality. Its strongest effect is felt by those born on the 10th, 20th or 30th of any month. The birthdays 19th and 28th also contain zeros in a concealed position since both numbers reduce to 10, giving added strength to the 1 vibration.

In the birth month (that is, only the 10th month), the zero's power to influence the personality is diminished considerably, so much so that it may be considered ineffective. In the birth year, where the vibratory influence of the numbers is the weakest, it has no power at all.

Limitations are placed on personalities with an abundance of zeros in their birth dates. The more zeros present, the fewer are the avenues available for expression.

The following are some examples of how a zero can or cannot influence a personality:

10 . 5 . 1976 Without a zero this birth date would in any case produce a self-confident and positive personality. The presence of the zero increases the strength of the 1 vibration giving it greater chances of success.

10 . 11 . 1911 The zero here is not advantageous since it merely increases the strength of an already rigid personality owing to an excess of the 1 vibration. Many negative traits of the 1 will appear.

30 . 8 . 1936   This birth date, even without the zero, produces a personality inclined towards negativity and with an inferiority complex. The zero aggravates the situation.

20 . 2 . 1952   The negativity of a Two personality is increased by the zero.

15 . 10 . 1934   The zero in this position has no effect on a strong-willed and positive personality.

3 . 3 . 1940   The zero does not do anything to increase the negativity of an already negative Three personality since it occupies the weakest position in the birth date.

THE SECOND SPHERE OF INFLUENCE
THE BIRTH DATE TOTALLED

The next number which possesses a strong, independent function is the single digit arrived at by totalling the numbers of the birth date. This forms the Second Sphere of Influence. For example, the birth date 17 . 6 . 1927 is simply added across, as follows: $1 + 7 + 6 + 1 + 9 + 2 + 7 = 33$. The multiple number is again added: $3 + 3 = 6$. The Second Sphere of Influence for this birth date will be governed by the 6 vibration. The Master vibrations 11 and 22 are not reduced to 2 and 4 respectively but remain as 11 and 22 as the following examples illustrate: 13 . 11 . 1958 = 29 = 11, and 10 . 10 . 1955 = 22.

The single number or Master number obtained as suggested holds the combined force of all the numbers of the birth date, thus giving it considerable power and is regarded by numerologists as the key that discloses the purpose behind an individual's existence. It is known by many names, such as the Destiny Number, the Life Path Number, the Number of Fate, the Ruling Number, the Birth Force Number and the Life's Lesson Number. All these names, while giving a clear description, carry essentially the same meaning. The most popular ones, however, are the Destiny Number and the Life Path Number.

Seen as the Destiny Number, or the Number of Fate, it indicates the reason and purpose of our birth and shows the directions in which we should guide our development and the type of work we are best equipped by nature to undertake. If it is considered as our Ruling Number or Birth Force Number, it indicates the type of power or energy with which we have been endowed and which is to be used throughout our life span. As the Life's Lesson Number it points out the lessons we have come into this life to learn, the adjustments to be made and personal qualities to be acquired.

To summarise, the Destiny Number, or the Second Sphere of Influence, indicates on the one hand the need to recognise and acquire and adapt ourselves to the personal qualities of this vibration, and on the other hand to choose our vocations and hobbies in the directions pointed out by this number. To aid us in doing so there is a natural pull or push, as the case may be, in the direction of this vibration's characteristics. Personality traits found in the First Sphere of Influence that are complementary to the requirements of the Second Sphere would naturally make life smoother, whereas such traits that conflict with the Destiny Number would suggest greater difficulties, adjustments and challenges.

People who are aware of their Destiny Number and its "call" and who consciously steer themselves in its direction should find greater fulfilment than those who are unaware of this Sphere of Influence on their lives and who, as a result, just drift along. This is the number that is given to someone who asks "What is my number?". It is regarded as a person's "lucky" number. Although a number cannot really be considered to be lucky or unlucky, it may certainly have great significance in our lives. The Destiny Number is often found associated in some way or the other in the many and varied functions and events in our lives. It frequently turns up in dates of important personal events, in names of close relatives, places, and even in material possessions such as house numbers, car numbers, important personal documents and sums of money. To this extent at least it will be seen that the Destiny Number, as its name implies, has an influence on our lives. It is recommended by numerologists that this number be consciously used for important events and other activities.

Furthermore, if the Destiny Number does not show up at all times, other numbers that are in harmony with it will do so. These can also be used in lieu of or in addition to the Destiny Number. If the 6 in our example does not always appear, invariably a 3 or a 9, which are in harmony with the 6, will do so. The following is a list of numbers that are in harmony with each other. They may be used or regarded as alternatives, not only in this sphere of destiny, but in other areas as well.

Number 1   3, 5, 7
Number 2   4, 8

Number 3 1, 5, 6, 9
Number 4 2, 8
Number 5 1, 3, 7
Number 6 3, 9
Number 7 1, 3, 5
Number 8 2, 4
Number 9 3, 6

The analysis on the following pages reveals the major purpose of our lives according to our Destiny Number. As adults, many of the points should be familiar to us. If they are not, there is a great deal of unfulfilled potential in our lives that could bring us happiness and satisfaction. If there are aspects discussed that we have never or rarely used in our lives, we are invited to explore them and they could become areas that could be used to enrich our lives and bring greater happiness and satisfaction.

Young people especially, or those analysing the destiny of a child, are in a position to choose the course or direction which should bring the greatest rewards. People are not placed on earth to forever blunder and stumble without direction or purpose. Numerologists and adherents of various schools of philosophy and religions believe that we are given existence so we may learn particular lessons and achieve recognisable aims. These lessons and aims are directly linked to the unique personality traits and destiny which are offered to us by the numbers of our birth date and name. As we gain moral and spiritual understanding while dealing with the challenges of our identity and our lives, we develop as human beings and make a contribution to the evolution of society. Fulfilling our destiny is the surest way to achieve these personal rewards. This book encourages us to seek these rewards.

VIBRATION NUMBER *1* AS DESTINY

As individuality is the hallmark of this vibration, a course of individual thought and action is called for. Subjects of this Life Path will strive for independence, with the conviction that their future lies in their own hands. Success will be achieved by following the development of such qualities as self-confidence, self-sufficiency and self-reliance. Dependence and expectation of support from others will be avoided. These people may leave home early and lead independent lives but family loyalty will remain strong. They will rely on their own judgement and develop the capacity to overcome obstacles that lie in the way of personal achievement. Friendships will be restricted to a few old and trusted companions.

Other qualities that will come to the fore and should be encouraged are willpower, self-control, courage, originality, initiative, creativity and leadership. The development and use of these qualities should, in the first instance, be used to control and govern the individuals themselves, before they are used in positions of authority and leadership to direct others.

However, a 1 destiny does not automatically indicate a role of leader. The alternative to this role is the state of the individualist or loner who will avoid both subordinate and authoritative roles in life and remain just his or her own person. The forces of this destiny will push these personalities to act in such a manner that they remove themselves from restricting, subordinate and subservient positions. It is not the destiny of the follower or the collaborator.

The principal motivating force will be the desire for personal advancement. Self will be placed before others. Whether care will be taken to do so without hurting or causing injustice will depend on other Spheres of Influence. The subjects of this destiny should realise that a cooperative spirit can be acquired without losing one's individuality.

People favoured by this destiny are unconventional and will frequently break away and set their own patterns of behaviour and will not tolerate interference and criticism. These patterns are usually followed by others who look to these people to set new standards. Their originality and creativity will be confined to the physical plane. The degree and direction to which this strong destiny will be fulfilled must of course depend upon the strength of the personality type as shown in the First Sphere of Influence. This important fact, which also applies to all other destiny numbers, must be kept in mind.

If a 1 destiny is combined with a negative personality, especially a negative One, Four or Eight personality, the subjects will tend to be dictatorial, strongly egotistical, overconfident, selfish, hypersensitive, boastful and set in their ways. The birth date 4 . 4 . 1946 = 28 = 10 = 1 is an example.

VIBRATION NUMBER *2* AS DESTINY

The 2 destiny is the direct opposite of the 1. While people with a 1 destiny turn out to be leaders, loners or masters of their own lives, people with a 2 destiny are inclined to enter into associations, fraternities and partnerships. They take a supportive role and enjoy communal living. Also, while egoism is the chief personal trait of the 1, the 2 destiny makes no demands for a display of ego, which is usually submerged in the service of a leader or an organisation.

The positive Twos will develop a self-sufficiency and inner composure that will remove the need to promote their individuality and will give them the ability to work as a power and influence behind the scenes. The "king makers" of politics or the "powers behind the throne" are usually those with 2 destinies. To elaborate on this facet of the 2 vibration, let us take a glimpse into the inner meaning of numbers. The 2 vibration, as mentioned earlier, is the primary receptive force with a negative polarity. The word negative is used in its electrical sense and means "force that does not act but draws to itself and retains power through magnetic attraction". The 2 vibration is really a reserve force or storehouse of power.

Success is also achieved in diplomacy, mediation, negotiation and peacemaking. In any of these functions the Twos may occupy positions of personal power, authority and direct influence. All Twos are well advised to concentrate on development of willpower, decision making, the power of silence and the value of the most careful choice of the spoken word. Essentially, the 2 Life Path is one of giving rather than receiving, particularly the giving of self in service to others. This the Twos do willingly and in return receive ample reward in accordance with the law of compensation and the law of attraction.

They are drawn towards group activity where they display adaptability, agreeability and friendliness. A conventional lifestyle and traditional values appeal most to these people and the principal motivating force behind their destiny is the need to establish tranquillity in their surroundings. As the path of marriage, companionship and association, a lonely life is not the lot of those with this destiny. They cannot and will not remain single. Social problems will be non-existent unless the personality type as shown in the First Sphere of Influence is oversensitive and therefore easily hurt.

A 2 destiny combined with a negative Two personality, such as 2 . 2 . 1924 = 20 = 2, is likely to involve the individual in several emotional affairs accompanied by heartache and failure. A desperate need for security and companionship may drive such a personality into a hasty and ill-advised marriage. Psychosomatic illnesses will cause problems, resulting in the development of a dreary and wailing type of personality.

VIBRATION NUMBER 3 AS DESTINY

The 3 destiny with its vibrations of freshness and vigour leads its subjects into the lighter and brighter sides of life, giving them a constant urge for self-expression in these areas. As versatility is one of the distinguishing features of this vibration, self-expression takes several forms.

Being essentially happy and optimistic extroverts, social involvement will be a high priority in their lives. A wide range of friends and acquaintances will be cultivated and social popularity and success enjoyed as a natural result. They will have the responsibility for inspiring and motivating people who come into contact with them. Endowed with the gift of entertainment and a genuine sense of humour, they will seek to hold the centre of attention in order to find fulfilment. Their best expression will be through the spoken word, while singing, acting and writing will also be avenues of expression that will be used.

Occupations and hobbies chosen will invariably be those that will allow their artistic talents to be displayed. Love of beauty, colour and music will influence their lives, often at the expense of practical and mundane responsibilities. New and unconventional ideas will often bring them into conflict with the established order of society. This is not a destiny that will seek comfort and security in a quiet domestic scene. Domestic responsibilities should not be allowed to hold back these people, for self-expression on as wide a scale as possible, which is the essence of the 3 vibration, will always be their strongest need.

Combined with a negative personality, this destiny will produce negative qualities of self-absorption, criticism, intolerance and strong escapist tendencies. There will also be a strong demand for constant emotional attention from others without a similar response being given by them. The birth date 3 . 3 . 1977 = 30 = 3 is an example.

VIBRATION NUMBER 4 AS DESTINY

Whereas the energies of the 3 are concentrated on the mental and artistic realms of life, those of the 4 will be firmly directed towards the establishment of a solid foundation on the physical side of life with a practical and commonsense approach. The field of activity of the Fours will not be wide, adventuresome and colourful, but will be concentrated on a few projects requiring physical work and practical application. Emphasis will be placed on material acquisitions with a sound sense of values guiding them. Money will be spent judiciously and an appreciable amount will always be set aside for the future. The gambler will not be found with this destiny.

Fours develop early in life the qualities of responsibility, duty, loyalty and dependability. As service to the community is the forte of these people, many demands are made by others on their time and energy, and their talents are put to constant use. Governed in this sphere by the vibration that produces the builders of social order and upholders of the establishment and tradition, they soon become known as the solid citizens of their community.

This is a stay-put vibration and herein lies its strength. It will not be easy to pursuade a Four to change direction once set on a chosen course. Travel is not part of this destiny and Fours usually find themselves too busy to indulge in this pastime. They may be subject to the danger of becoming too absorbed in work and should be advised to seek periods of relaxation away from work and responsibilities. A sense of humour and imagination are not strong qualities of this vibration and attempts should be made to develop these qualities.

Negative people with this destiny are dull and dreary and very likely fall into a rut and be content to remain there. They are extremely reluctant to part with their money and possessions and may find themselves in a situation where they do not possess their wealth but their wealth possesses them. The birth date 6 . 6 . 1936 = 31 = 4 is an example.

VIBRATION NUMBER 5 AS DESTINY

Freedom is the watchword of this destiny and those subject to it will strive to acquire freedom of thought, speech and action and to learn the responsible use of these possessions. They may expect change, variety and travel in their lives. Adaptability and flexibility will be required of them to cope with the many unexpected changes that will take place. This is a destiny of growth and advancement through adaptation and willingness to let go of the old for the new.

Fives regard life as an adventure to be experienced with enthusiasm and energy. They live each day with a greater degree of intensity than those with other Life Paths. Due to the comprehensive nature of their outlook they are soon able to feel at home wherever they are and adapt to all types of people and customs.

Young people with this vibration as their destiny become

sullen and uncooperative if restricted and will rebel against authority. Freedom fighters, whether religious, political, social or otherwise, are most often subjects of this destiny.

These people should concentrate on developing quality and power of speech, for their potential in this area is considerable. They must, however, guard against the natural tendency of subjects of the 5 vibration to speak out with assumed authority on matters of which they have no specialised knowledge. Proficiency in foreign languages is more easily acquired by this vibration than by others.

In order to succeed in business, they will need to develop concentration, self-discipline and attention to detail. This destiny gives its subjects the opportunity to express a wide variety of talent, but some negative qualities such as restlessness, impulsiveness and self-indulgence should be brought under control.

Combined with a negative personality type, especially a negative Five, such as 5 . 5 . 1948 = 32 = 5, misuse of freedom can become a real danger, plus self-indulgence in sensuality, drink, drugs and gambling.

VIBRATION NUMBER 6 AS DESTINY

People with this destiny steer their lives in the direction of the general qualities of the 6 vibration. It is known as the path of responsibility, particularly in the domestic, social and humanitarian fields. While on the one hand there is a strong pull towards these responsibilities, on the other hand most of these people will need to prepare themselves to assume such responsibilities by making changes in their personal attitudes and lifestyle. The need to make many personal adjustments before this destiny is fulfilled is clearly indicated. They should learn not to look for perfection but to adjust to and accept circumstances and people as they find them. As their first priority, they will seek to establish harmony, comfort and beauty in the domestic scene.

The well-developed artistic appreciation of this vibration is reflected in the furnishings and decoration of their homes. They may also become connoisseurs of wine, good food and works of art. Having secured domestic felicity and personal balance, they will turn their attention to community needs, especially as counsellors, teachers, guides and peacemakers.

They are rarely critical and condemnatory, and those who have fully set themselves on this path of humanitarian service will submerge their own egos in order to build up the deflated and bruised egos of others. Love of the physical and spiritual aspects of life will operate with equal force. It is this characteristic that makes them accessible and credible counsellors to people of all ages seeking stability in their lives. More than others, these Sixes are able to teach the meaning of love and understanding, which they invariably do by personal example.

A negative person with this destiny is domineering, unreasonable, overpossessive and jealous, especially in regard to domestic issues. Their constant whining, nagging and faultfinding will make life difficult for their partners. Someone with a birth date such as 2 . 6 . 1960 = 24 = 6 may be subject to this type of negativity.

VIBRATION NUMBER 7 AS DESTINY

This is a Life Path where the mind is used to effect a transfer of interests from the material and physical realms to the abstract and subtle. It does not, however, indicate that those subject to it should cease to engage in the affairs of the world but that they should acquire the wisdom to look upon all material possessions with detachment. While this attitude of non-attachment to material possessions is being developed, they may pursue their quest into the eternal truths of life. They will realise that these truths become known only to those who do not permit worldly possessions to enslave them. An infinite capacity to gather abstract knowledge awaits those who take up the challenge of this destiny. Their worldly activities will always be tinged with the wisdom they will acquire and their philosophical attitude will help them overcome their share of the disappointments and vicissitudes of life. They should be careful not to acquire superficial standards and should constantly examine their motives and maintain only enduring values.

A profession in a specialised field should be chosen that will allow the 7 vibration's power to investigate and analyse to be used. Their best work is carried out alone — or with very few fellow workers around — away from crowds, noise and commercial activity. They are better suited to become professionals than to enter the business world. However, those engaged in business enterprises are high principled and honest and will not indulge in unscrupulous competition.

Because the 7 vibration tends towards too much self-criticism and the pursuit of perfection, they need to establish harmony within themselves. Self-appreciation will lead to happier relationships with others as well. The tendency of Seven personalities to withhold their learning and wisdom, which results from their introverted natures, should be overcome. They should try to be more outgoing and to spread their knowledge among those in need.

Negative personalities with this destiny are certain to seek seclusion and various forms of escapism from the social and other mundane responsibilities. Birth dates such as 7 . 7 . 1973 = 34 = 7 and 2 . 2 . 1992 = 25 = 7 are examples.

VIBRATION NUMBER 8 AS DESTINY

The wide world of commerce, industry, government, organisations and corporations is the field of activity open to those with this destiny. It is by no means a domesticated or parochial Life Path, neither is it one for dreamers and visionaries. Their energies are directed towards success in the practical, managerial and financial affairs of life. Courage, ambition and dedication will be called for, and in turn given, by those on this Life Path. They will drive themselves hard and will not hesitate to drive others too.

In their pursuit of power and success in the material world they need to bear in mind that the 8 vibration also demands, as a consequence of its potential for success, the exercise of social and economic justice and benevolence. Unless a balance is struck between these responsibilities and obligations, the law of cause and effect will neutralise the success gained and fulfilment of this destiny will not be achieved. These people must be wary of the trap of materialism and power for power's sake.

Needless to say, not all Eights will reach the top of their chosen vocations, but their destiny indicates that they should strive to do so; the result will be advancement well beyond the average. Their field of endeavour could, for instance, range from management of a single supermarket to the management of a multinational company. Promotion will be automatic when their enthusiasm for work, practicality and energy are displayed and observed.

Most Eights will find themselves acting as counsellors in financial and economic affairs. As many people will look to them for guidance, they will need to remember the responsibilities thrust upon them by their positions of knowledge and authority. Unless supported by emotional numbers in the birth date, people with this destiny will have problems with emotional expression. Although compassionate and sympathetic, they will resent having to express these sentiments, especially if they happen to stand in the way of their public life. All Eights should be conscious of their dress and general appearance as an important aspect of their public image.

In a negative personality, especially a negative Four or Eight (for example, 4 . 8 . 1994 = 35 = 8), both mental and physical cruelty could erupt from time to time.

VIBRATION NUMBER *9* AS DESTINY

The fulfilment of the 9 destiny calls for the surrender of the personal for the impersonal. This destiny will be fulfilled to the extent that the individual is prepared to sublimate self-centredness for the welfare of humanity as a whole. The Brotherhood of Man should be the principal concern of these people. Every effort should be made to rise above the divisive prejudices of race, class and religion. All forms of separatism that contribute towards social and economic injustice and restrictions that hinder cultural intermingling of people should be eschewed.

This is a difficult destiny to follow and the extent of success achieved will depend largely on the personality type. Much self-adjustment is necessary and this may come about after suffering and disappointment, when the worthiness of this humanitarian Life Path may be accepted and followed. As this is not a destiny for quiet suburban or country living, strong Nine personalities who find themselves confined to this type of life will suffer much frustration and unhappiness. Freedom of movement will be sought after, not only for humanitarian activity but also for cultural advancement. Artistic talents could be carried to high levels of attainment. Keen spiritual awareness will find these people involved in metaphysics, mysticism and studies in comparative religions.

As this is by no means a domesticated Life Path, partners should allow these personalities considerable freedom of movement and reconcile themselves to the fact that the love of these Nines will reach out well beyond home, family and community. They will place no importance on material security and their energies will not be spent in this direction.

Negative personalities, such as those born on 9.9.1935 = 36 = 9, or 6.6.1995 = 36 = 9, are likely to be egocentric, moody, fickle, critical and ill-tempered. They will display a feeling of bitterness towards the world and project a facade of wisdom and knowledge which they do not possess.

VIBRATION NUMBER 11 AS DESTINY

Birth dates totalling 29 and 38 are offered this Master Vibration as their destiny. People who do not take up this offer will follow the destiny of the straightforward 2 vibration. However, for those who follow the 11 destiny, there is unlimited potential for personal advancement in metaphysical studies, development of clairvoyance, intuition and prophecy. It is not a destiny that calls for the pursuit of personal gain in terms of material wealth and power; it calls for the spiritual side of life to be awakened. Once this awakening takes place, these people should learn the practical application of their spiritual gains.

Elevens will invariably enter areas of activity that will not only facilitate spiritual growth but will also provide scope for the application of their higher values. The professions should be chosen rather than competition in business and commerce. The inventive genius of the 11 vibration will have wide opportunity in both the arts and sciences. Down-to-earth and practical associates will be of invaluable support to these Elevens, for such associates will bring about a fine balance between vision and inspiration on the one hand and commonsense and pragmatism on the other. They will also be able to place some restraint on the spontaneous generosity of the Elevens.

VIBRATION NUMBER 22 AS DESTINY

This is the most powerful of all Destiny vibrations, giving its subjects unlimited resources for expansion as master planners and master builders in all departments of human activity, especially those which leave behind lasting benefits for the welfare of mankind. Not many individuals with this Life Path are able to lift themselves to the peak of its vibratory power and meet the challenges that are offered. Those few who do soon become world renowned. The average Twenty-twos who avail themselves of the power of this Master vibration will invariably make a name for themselves in their chosen fields of activity.

This is a multi-talented vibration containing the features of all others, and those whose destiny is the number 22 may choose any field of endeavour and meet with success. Politics, business, the professions, government service and large humanitarian organisations are all open to them. Twenty-twos who are oblivious to the nature and power of their destiny will revert to the standard 4 destiny as solid, dependable citizens.

THE BIRTH MONTH AND THE BIRTH YEAR

To complete the analysis of the influences of the birth date, we will examine the numbers of the month and year of birth and their bearing on the personality as a whole.

THE BIRTH MONTH

The number or numbers of the birth month are not as strong as those of the birthday, nor do they possess an independent function or create personal identity as do the numbers of the birthday and the Destiny number. They work in conjunction with the other numbers of the birth date and influence them to act in either a favourable or unfavourable manner on the personality. They may provide an essential vibration, giving balance to the personality, or overload the vibratory structure of a personality with a vibration already existing quite strongly in the birthday. The 9th month, for instance, will contribute negative influences on a birth date such as $9.9.1935 = 36 = 9$, and favourable influences on a birth date such as $4.9.1941 = 28 = 10 = 1$. In the first example, a straightforward Nine personality is stifled by too many 9 characteristics, resulting in negative traits entering the personality. In the second example, the comprehensive 9 vibration opens out an unimaginative personality type.

    The birth month may have a single digit or a multiple number, as does the birthday, but to a lesser extent since only the 11th and 12th months have two digits. These are not reduced to a single 2 and a single 3 but in the 11th month are considered as two 1's and as a single 1 and a single 2 in the 12th month. The zero of the 10th month may be discounted since it does not have an appreciable influence on the personality from this position.

    Further examples of the influence of the number or numbers of the birth month are as follows:

$2.5.1955 = 27 = 9$.   The 5 vibration of the 5th month overloads the emotional aspects of a sentimental Two personality. Emotion has too strong a hold on this personality and will hinder the responsibilities of the 9 destiny.

$2.1.1955 = 23 = 5$.   The 1 vibration of the 1st month is strong enough to control emotionalism and give self-assurance to the Two personality and will also assist in coping with the 5 destiny.

$12.11.1933 = 21 = 3$.   The two 1's of the eleventh month add strength to an already strong Three personality. Self-consciousness and egocentricity are also increased. There will be no problems in fulfilling the 3 destiny.

12 . 8 . 1933 = 27 = 9. The 8 vibration of the 8th month draws the thought processes of the personality out of self-centredness and helps with the wide ranging 9 destiny.

3 . 12 . 1992 = 27 = 9. The 1 of the 12th month gives positivity to the Three personality and the 2 vibration extends the range of the artistic and social attributes.

22 . 1 . 1966 = 27 = 9. This is an outstanding example of a Master vibration controlling a positive personality. Positivity is gained through the 1 in the birth month.

4 . 2 . 1960 = 22. The energy and drive required for fulfilling this Master destiny will not be provided by the 2 in the birth month.

THE BIRTH YEAR

The numbers of the year of birth provide additional vibrations but do not have as strong an influence on the personality as the numbers of the birth month. They do, however, provide outlets for expression, and thereby balance, to the personality as a whole if they are not found in either the birthday or birth month. They may also contribute towards overloading of vibrations, as in the case of someone born on 3 . 3 . 1933. In common with the numbers of the birth month, these numbers are of a supportive and influential nature only and do not possess an independent function.

When analysing the variety of influences within a birth date, we need to recognise the relative importance of the position of the numbers and also the fact that when the same number reappears it has a weakening effect over the personality, leading to negative attitudes. This weakening takes place, however, when the repetition of a number is found in the stronger areas of the birth date, such as the birthday and birth month. In the example birth date of 3 . 3 . 1933 given in the previous paragraph, the two 3's in the birth year have merely aggravated an already negative birth date. They would not have done so if the birth date was 3.12.1933. In this case, the numbers of the birth month give balance to the personality and the two 3's of the birth year are not strong enough to override the power of the numbers of the birth month.

Two more examples illustrating the influence of the numbers of the birth year are:

24 . 4 . 1944 = 28 = 10 = 1.   The 4 vibration is too strong. Although this is a Six personality, many negative 4 influences control the individual. If these influences can be checked, the positive 4 qualities will help with the 1 destiny.

21 . 4 . 1944 = 25 = 7.   The 1, 2 and 3 vibrations control this personality with the help of the 4 in the birth month. The two 4's in the birth year will contribute, but not in a negative way since the 4 in the birth month does not control the personality.

The close relational influence of the birth month and birth year upon the fundamental personality type formed by the number or numbers of the birthday should be given serious attention before a final assessment of the personality type is made. This should be followed by observing their influence on the Destiny vibration through the personality type. The numbers of the birth month and birth year have a direct influence on the formation of the personality type and an indirect influence on the Destiny. It is the complete personality that is responsible for fulfilling the requirements of Destiny.

Further significance of these numbers will be seen in the next chapter where the numerological grid is demonstrated.

THE NUMEROLOGICAL GRID

The previous chapters, in which the First and Second Spheres of Influence were discussed, have largely illustrated the characteristics of the numbers as an independent function. However, as indicated, they are defined more specifically by their relationship with the other numbers in the birth date. A number of examples were given to highlight some significant interactions. It is this interaction, while creating positive, negative and neutralising influences, that contributes towards forming the complete personality and affecting Destiny.

In this chapter our aim is to develop an understanding of the outcome of these two Spheres of Influence operating simultaneously. In order to do so, it is necessary to study in detail the interrelation of numbers in the birth date. This is best done by first examining the degree of influence each number of the birth date has in forming the vibratory structure of the personality, and then considering the nature of the Destiny number. Having studied the characteristics of both spheres separately, our next step will be to look at them together as two interconnected parts of the composite personality.

The easiest way to depict the First and Second Spheres of Influence as portrayed by the birth date is through the use of a simple numerological grid formed by horizontal and vertical lines. A complete grid with all the single numbers in their permanent positions is as follows:

3	6	9	Mental Plane
2	5	8	Emotional Plane
1	4	7	Physical Plane

The zero, lacking qualities of its own, may be placed for convenience sake with the 1. Needless to say, there is no birth date that will fill all the squares of the grid.

The three horizontal planes are levels of expression of the qualities of the numbers shown thereon. This is, however, a general classification since most vibrations share some common characteristics, though they express them differently. The following is a more detailed classification and should be kept in mind when considering the grid:

Number 1 Physical/Mental
Number 2 Emotional/Intuitional
Number 3 Mental/Emotional
Number 4 Physical
Number 5 Emotional/Physical/Mental/Intuitional
Number 6 Mental
Number 7 Physical/Intuitional
Number 8 Emotional/Mental
Number 9 Mental/Intuitional/Emotional

It is a mistake to imagine that the numbers of one plane are more desirable or superior to another. These planes indicate methods of expression — the impulses that reveal not only thought and feeling but personality traits and tendencies. Above all, they indicate the area or areas where the greatest amount of power is concentrated. This can be seen at a glance once the numbers of a birth date are correctly placed within the grid.

The area of power forms the individual's personality type. When this is known, the first important comparison can be made and the relationship between the First and Second Spheres of Influence becomes evident. For example, if the power base of the First Sphere is on the physical plane and the Second Sphere is also in the direction of physical plane development and activities, the establishment of a successful lifestyle should not meet with many difficulties. On the other hand, if the First Sphere is on the emotional plane and the Second on the physical plane, there is bound to be inner conflict on account of personal adjustments needed for fulfilling the requirements of Destiny.

Mind governs the mental plane. Everything is referred to the mind before action and reaction. People on the emotional plane refer all things to their emotions in the first instance; the heart governs the personality. Those governed by the physical plane have their thought processes geared towards the body and practical earthly undertakings. A down-to-earth form of thinking governs these people. Finally, those with intuitional vibrations will learn to trust their instincts and premonitions.

Spirituality, the element in mankind concerned with divinity, spirit, soul and the part of life regarded as immortal, is a power that is spread throughout all vibrations. Each number, with its intrinsic qualities, channels the spiritual element through the personality according to the nature of its qualities. For example, some personalities fulfil their spirituality through worship, others through service and still others through concentration and meditation. Spirituality is expressed and displayed through the traits of the strongest vibrations, or through any one or more of the Six Spheres of Influence.

The lack of numbers on the mental plane, excepting the century 9 which all birth dates have, does not indicate that the individual has no mental capacity. It merely shows that the mind is directed towards emotional or physical pursuits, where high intelligence and initiative may be displayed.

Similarly, the absence of emotional plane numbers does not mean that emotion is lacking. There is as much emotion and feeling within the personality as one with emotional numbers but the outlets for display and demonstration of emotional qualities may not be available. Such personalities may appear to have greater control over their feelings by not displaying outward emotional reaction, though they could be seething with emotion within. They may resort to defensive or evasive behaviour in order to cope with their inability to give natural expression to their feelings. This usually results in restriction of intimate expression, leading to misunderstanding by others. Body contact in the form of spontaneous embraces, hugs and other forms of endearment will be distasteful to their nature. These people will undoubtedly be loving, yet seemingly incapable of expressing their love. Demonstration of emotion may not be considered as important and necessary by some of this group.

Those individuals with only the century number 1 on the physical plane have no interest or aptitude in the physical side of life, unless support is given through the Fourth Sphere of Influence where the appropriate talents are found. The mind is generally used instead on the mental or emotional levels, or both, according to the type of birth date.

Thought processes of individuals with vibrations predominantly confined to one or more of these planes will project them into action appropriate to the qualities of that plane or planes. On the other hand, individuals with mixed numbers will have little difficulty in functioning confidently and naturally on any two or more of these planes.

Finally, the 5 vibration, although a strongly emotional one, is nevertheless the only vibration that gives expression on all three planes, plus the intuitional level. A number 5 in the birthday or birth month has a stabilising influence on the personality as a whole because of its multiplicity of expression. A 5 name will be most helpful to someone with an excess of numbers on either the mental or physical plane, or for one with no numbers on the emotional plane.

Vibrations usually form themselves into three other categories, which in turn place people under their influence into three further fundamental types. This can be seen in the areas formed by the vertical lines of the grid. Numbers 1, 2 and 3 represent vibrations of individuality and the thought processes of individuals under their influence are oriented towards self and self-interests. The pronouns I, me and mine figure largely in their thoughts, speech and actions. The "I" or "me first" attitude is a common feature of these personalities. Objective consideration of issues is foreign to their nature. Originality is the principal characteristic displayed by the thoughts of the Ones, fantasy by the Twos and creative imagination by the Threes.

The vibratory influences of the numbers 4, 5 and 6 give an added community consciousness. These are regarded as numbers of action. The thought processes of subjects of these numbers project out of self into the community. The down-to-earth labour of the Fours, the intense nervous energy of the Fives and the constant mental activity of the Sixes are further distinguishing features.

The numbers 7, 8 and 9 denote power and widespread influence, giving their subjects an increased orientation towards international consciousness. This power is found in the spiritual depth of the Sevens, the authority and justice of the Eights and the humanitarianism of the Nines.

EXAMINING THE GRID

Once a grid picture has been constructed by placing the numbers of a given birth date in their correct positions and the First and Second Spheres of Influence highlighted, preliminary work on the personality may begin.

1. Look for the area or areas of power in the planes of expression. An evenly distributed set of numbers will indicate ability to motivate on any two or more planes. A set of numbers with the base of power confined to one plane will indicate whether the individual is essentially physically, emotionally or mentally oriented. However, secondary characteristics may be revealed with numbers on other planes and the degree to which a secondary nature exists should be noted. A mentally oriented person, for instance, may possess secondary characteristics on the emotional plane, as in the case of a birth date such as 12 . 9 . 1980 = 30 = 3. This birth date should be considered from the mental level with a secondary approach from the emotional plane. A lopsided set of numbers with heavy overloading on any one plane, or the repetition of a single number, indicates a closed-in and negative personality. By the same token, this situation could also produce genius; that is, one who has or may pursue a course of action indicated by the governing vibration to extraordinary limits at the expense of other considerations of life. This eventuality is, however, more the exception than the rule.

2. Note the absence of a number in the squares of a particular plane. This important point indicates that the individual under examination has no outlets for self-expression on this particular plane. It is by no means an area of power. At the same time, it is also advisable to note all other blanks in the grid because these reveal that the birth date has not supplied the individual with the qualities peculiar to the missing vibration.

3. Next, observe the vertical squares in their order. Consciousness of self is emphasised in the area covered by the 1, 2 and 3 vibrations, while community consciousness is added to the 4, 5 and 6 vibrations. A global awareness is characteristic of the 7, 8 and 9 vibrations. Here again, balanced or one-sided personalities can be seen.

4. The blanks in both the horizontal and vertical sections should be carefully noted, not only as areas revealing lack of power and expression, but also as areas to be concentrated on when the next four Spheres of Influence are examined. The whole name, within which these four spheres operate, often provides balancing vibrations. However, if no help is available from the names, these blank areas will remain as weaknesses to be concentrated upon and developed as well as possible through life.

5. Once the power base and weak areas have been established, the next important factor that can be recorded is the degree of positivity or negativity that exists within the personality. The determining factor will be the presence or absence of the 1 vibration. Willpower, self-assurance and self-control, which are the outstanding qualities of this vibration, should be looked for since it is these qualities principally that contribute towards determining a positive personality or a negative one. However, it is advisable to suspend final judgement until the four Spheres of Influence within the whole name have been examined.

6. The Second Sphere of Influence, or the Destiny number, should be considered on its own in the first instance. Once the attractions, directions and lessons indicated by this sphere have been established, it should be reconsidered in relation to the First Sphere or the personality type. The directions in which the Destiny of the individual point, in regard to vocations and other activities in life, should be noted first. Next, the lessons to be learned and the qualities of character to be acquired should be observed. Finally, the essential step may be taken of observing whether the personality type as formed by the birthday and supporting numbers assist in fulfilling what is required by the Destiny number. In short, whether the First Sphere of Influence complements the Second Sphere or whether there is conflict. An easy life or a personal battle will be indicated by the answers.

7. There are active vibrations representing expenditure of energy and receptive vibrations representing storage of energy. The odd numbers are the active and the even numbers are the receptive. Whatever sex is being considered in a numerological analysis, it is always very interesting to observe which numbers predominate. The odd numbers are also inspirational and freedom loving, whereas the evens are practical and home loving. For instance, a female with active odd numbers predominating will hardly be the coy, domesticated and motherly type. If her social status permits, she will be an ambitious career person with strong leadership and creative tendencies. If she has a birth date such as $10.5.1930 = 19 = 10 = 1$, family and society should not confine her to domesticity since this birth date will produce a competitive and authoritative individual. On the other hand, a male with receptive even numbers, such as 6 . 2 . 1924 = 24 = 6, will by nature be non-competitive, placid, domesticated and non-aggressive. Given a choice, in many instances he would rather be the homemaker than the provider. Furthermore, if these two people were to enter into marriage or any other long-term partnership, there is no doubt that the female will take charge and the male will be quite happy to let her do so.

The grid can also be an easy reference to particular characteristics of the personality being analysed. The points that follow are a guide to some of many significant personality traits that can be seen. They will assist in a systematic examination and will also be useful when the grids of two or more people are being examined. There is no limit to the personality traits that we can look for. The extent of our search will depend on the degree of our curiosity and use of our imagination. While some characteristics will be conspicuous others will be concealed or qualified. The grid may be regarded as a puzzle to be unravelled. The challenge should not be taken up in haste, for some experience is needed before we can develop the expertise to unlock all the secrets the grid can reveal.

8. The grid pattern can show whether or not an individual under examination is an extrovert. This is not only a very interesting aspect of a personality but an important one to know. People have various types and degrees of extroversion. Almost all vibrations, whether on the positive or negative side, favour this facet of the human personality owing to the gregarious nature of mankind. A close study of the nature of all vibrations will reveal the type of extroversion peculiar to a given birth date. For instance, a Two personality is an extrovert who enoys group activity but prefers to remain in the background. Three and Five personalities are also extroverts but these demand the centre of attention and prefer the foreground of activity. The Seven personality, being a quiet, contemplative type, will display this trait in small well-controlled doses. The continued extroversion of a Seven personality cannot be taken for granted.

Once again, the presence or absence of the 1 vibration will influence the degree and quality of extroversion. An aggressive type of extroversion may be found in a negative birth date, such as 8 . 4 . 1988 = 38 = 11, while a well-adjusted form will be displayed if the personality is born on 18.2.1988 = 37 = 10 = 1. Excessive shyness and sensitivity will be problems with some-

one born on 20.6.1969 = 33 = 6, although this person will always
need company. These problems will not be present in someone
born a day later. The 1 vibration of the 21st would overcome
shyness and, along with the underlying 3 vibration, bring about
a more active form of extroversion.

Introverted personalities are rare when compared to the
extroverts. A close study of all areas of influence should be made
and considerable thought given before labelling someone an
introvert. Many a hastily classified introvert may be crying out
for the right sort of company. Natural introverts may be produced by the 1 vibration or the 7 and these people could be
adopting a positive form of introversion where they just prefer
their own company to the company of others.

9. The quality of competitiveness has become increasingly
important in every aspect of life. The ability to compete in sport,
public life and other areas, and the extent to which the competitive spirit prevails, should be ascertained. Quite often, an essentially non-competitive character may be found, for there are
many that fall into this category. The ability to pick the presence
or absence of a competitive spirit in a particular area of activity
is a grave responsibility held by parents and guardians. They
should examine this quality in a child before forcing or influencing it into an area of activity where strong competition is needed.
The absence of a competitive spirit, in the generally accepted
sense, in a particular field of activity should be noted and respected and should not be regarded as a detriment to success in
life.

The competitive spirit is found among the odd numbers. The 1, 3 and 5 vibrations make strong competitors, while
those influenced by the 7 and 9 are only mildly interested in
competition.

The even numbers are non-competitive, with the exception of the 8 which falls firmly into the strongly competitive
category. The 2 and 6 are the least interested in any form of
competition, while the 4 can be persuaded into competition and
often succeeds through sheer strength of purpose.

The birth dates 18.10.1951 = 26 = 8 and 15.8.1958 =
37 = 10 = 1 should produce strong competitors in all departments
of activity, while those born on birth dates such as 20.6.1963 =
27 = 9 and 6.4.1963 = 29 = 11 will show a great dislike for competition.

10. The possession of a money sense is a desirable asset for
success in our largely materialistic society. The numbers will
clearly show a capacity to spend money responsibly, to save and

invest, or the complete inability to save. The really tight-fisted ones can also be seen.

The vibrations 1, 7 and 8 provide the capacity to acquire and increase money reserves in personal and business affairs. Birth dates such as 17 . 1 . 1948 = 31 = 4 and 8 . 11 . 1994 = 33 = 6 exhibit this capacity. People with the 4 vibration governing them are the most cautious in their spending habits and are, in turn, the best savers. Subjects of the 3, 5 and 9 vibrations are the free spenders. They have no attachment to money for its own sake, but use it as a means of enjoying life. Nine personalities in particular are easily persuaded to part with their money and experience no qualms when doing so. Very little or no money reserves will be held by people born on such birth dates as 3 . 5 . 1950 = 23 = 5 or 9 . 5 . 1959 = 38 = 11. The Six personality stands out with a well-balanced attitude towards the acquisition and accumulation of money. Their books are always balanced and income usually exceeds expenditure. Subjects of the 2 vibration are fond of spending, but fear of the future holds them back to some extent. Their expenditure could often exceed their income, as they could be driven by impulse.

11. Domesticity may be regarded as a fundamental facet of our personality and ascertaining the degree in which it exists in an individual is always an interesting exercise and reveals many surprises. The old custom of the male being the wage earner and the female being the homemaker is being challenged while we work towards equality of the sexes. Numerology clearly shows that it is the vibratory makeup alone and not the sex that divides individuals into career persons, domesticated ones and the many that are in between.

As mentioned in Chapter 3, the vibration of domesticity is represented by the number 6 and people with this number controlling their First Sphere of Influence are the real home lovers. Attachment to home is a characteristic also shared by subjects of the 2 and 4 vibrations. Seven personalities can also settle down to a domestic way of life if their need for peace and quiet is found in the home.

The even numbers produce the home-oriented ones while the odd numbers create the outgoing ones not given to domesticity and a quiet family life. People born on birth dates such as 5 . 12 . 1935 = 26 = 8 or 8 . 1 . 1952 = 26 = 8, whether male or female, will be more inclined to follow a career in public life than be confined to domestic duties.

12. Oral expression is seen in many interesting forms depending on the personality type or the First Sphere of Influence.

Generally speaking, the Three and Five personalities are the impulsive talkers. The taciturn ones are the Ones and Sevens, while the genuine conversationalists are the Sixes, Nines and Twenty-twos. The authoritative ones are the Ones, Fives and Eights. The shy ones who speak only when they are addressed are the Twos, while the quiet ones who speak only when they have something worthwhile to say are the Fours. The Ones and Sevens also fall into this last group and are at ease when they speak on their speciality. The Elevens enjoy giving their points of view to all and sundry. A Five will be ready to speak about any subject, irrespective of any specialised knowledge, and the temporary enthusiasm they display is soon lost once the subject is closed. The argumentative ones are found among the Sixes, who are also the best story-tellers. Ones, Fours, Sevens and Eights are forthright and brief in speech and people who possess an intensification of these vibrations can be curt and peremptory.

So far, personal characteristics and potential have been examined but no consideration has been given to heredity and environmental conditioning. There is no doubt that these factors contribute to enhance, obscure, inhibit and generally influence, for good or ill, our individuality. The growing psyche of the child is shaped and moulded by its family, community and nation according to the customs and norms prevailing at the time of its growth. We can hardly escape this conditioning, but it must be understood as something apart from the real individual. Fortunately, with the growth of the personality we often outgrow this conditioning, allowing our real selves to blossom forth. There may be some, however, who fail to do so, for fear, ignorance of self and lethargy may have taken over. These unfortunate people may see out their lives unaware of their birthright of many-sided potential. Whenever something of a person's background is known, therefore, we should try to determine the degree of individuality and the degree of submission to this conditioning.

Since individuals under examination are at various stages of personal growth, it will often be observed that they do not conform to the complete picture presented by the chart. Whatever is found lacking, however, remains in potential. Furthermore, it will help us to remember that mankind is laboriously following a path of progress and our position on this path is determined by our degree of personal growth.

The vibratory powers of numbers are expressed on higher

or lower levels according to the development of the individual under their special influence or, we may say, the evolutionary status of the individual. They are used only to the degree to which the individual is capable of receiving them. Two people could have the same birth date, but the one who is further ahead on the evolutionary path will make fuller use of the power of his or her numbers. The worthiness of our thoughts, actions and reactions is therefore relative to our position on this path of progress.

NEGATIVITY

The state or condition of negativity is simply one in which positive attributes are not present and consequently individuals in this condition, instead of thinking and acting according to their best characteristics, resort to the negative aspects of their governing vibrations. Negativity is determined in two ways. First, by the absence of the number 1 in the birth date, and secondly, by the abundance of a particular number in the birth date. It may be expressed in either a passive or an active form.

Individuals suffering from varying degrees of negativity because of the absence of the 1 vibration in their birth dates exceed by far those with an excess of a single number. The number 1 which all birth dates have during this century may be discounted since it is in too weak a position to influence the personality. Although the form of negativity in this first category is related to the governing vibrations, certain common features are shared by these personalities, such as a lack of self-confidence leading to an inferiority complex and a strong inclination to underestimate and undersell themselves. The fuel of the 1 vibration is wanting, which should be activating these personalities to make full use of the talents of their numbers. More often than not these people possess an even distribution of numbers and as a result multiple talents are indicated. For all that, they would deny having them and show surprise and disbelief when their potential and capabilities are pointed out to them. Some typical birth dates with these problems are $23.6.1948 = 33 = 6$, $27.9.1948 = 40 = 4$ and $5.3.1948 = 30 = 3$.

People with the type of negativity in the first group are pleasant and likeable since they do not possess the disagreeable traits of egotism, aggressiveness, egocentricity and pride. Any harm they may do will be to themselves and not to others and such damage will be the result of omission rather than commission. All is not lost, however, in this form of negativity, for compensation can be found or made in the names, particularly in the free choice of the given name.

The 1 vibration governing the Third Sphere of Influence, with its constant and powerful rays is bound to give the required lift to the personality through its direct influence on the whole vibratory structure of the personality. The urge to forge ahead will constantly be experienced with the 1 vibration governing the vowels in the Fifth Sphere of Influence and, depending on the nature of environmental conditioning, these people will sooner or later overcome negative attitudes. The consonants of the Sixth Sphere, if governed by the 1 vibration, can be used up to a point but will not help in the long run, unless backed up by this number in other controlling spheres. The 1 vibration in the Fourth Sphere of Expression will be helpful since it will provide ease of expression of talents in occupational areas. Finally, the possession of three or more letters converting to the number 1 (A, J, S) in the whole name will compensate to an appreciable extent the drive and self-confidence not found in the birth date. This point is elaborated on in Chapter 10.

Total negativity, therefore, is not common in this group. Furthermore, personalities who are not assisted by a strong 1 vibration in any of the controlling Spheres of Influence may be guided and uplifted by a good upbringing and environment. The opposite is also true, unfortunately, for they are easily influenced or put down. The nature and degree of influence, good or bad, to which they will be susceptible will depend on the nature of the controlling numbers of the First Sphere of Influence.

In the second group negativity is caused by a repetition of a particular number in the birth date. Some examples are: 22 . 2 . 1920, 7 . 7 . 1977 and 4 . 4 . 1948. These situations lead to a weakening of the governing vibrations and to a more troublesome form of negativity — troublesome not only to the individuals affected but to others as well.

The number 1 is the only exception to this weakening process through repetition. Instead, this vibration strengthens itself and creates its own form of negativity by its very strength. Negative attitudes, however, do not exist unless the birth date is really overloaded, such as 11.11.1911 or 1.11.1910. Rigidity becomes the problem in these cases. Also, a strong defensive attitude is taken in relationships with others. This defensiveness takes the form of automatic self-justification whenever a casual or totally objective statement, enquiry or suggestion is made by someone. People with these birth dates are experts at instantly justifying their actions and reactions.

This second form of negativity can also be helped by the vibrations of one or more of the four Spheres of Influence within the names. However, the mitigating power will not be as strong as in the first category, owing to the concentration and closing in of negative traits within a single vibration. Some help can also be obtained from a whole name which gives a good all-round balance of numbers which the birth date lacks, as in the following example:

Birth date: 4 . 4 . 1940 = 22

C	A	R	O	L	I	N	E		J	A	Y	N	E		M	A	C	I	N	T	O	S	H
3	1	9	6	3	9	5	5		1	1	7	5	5		4	1	3	9	5	2	6	1	8

Vibration	Quantity
1	5
2	1
3	3
4	1
5	5
6	2
7	1
8	1
9	3

Our example shows that there are five letters with the 1 vibration, one letter with the 2 vibration and so on up to the 9 vibration. When these vibrations are placed in the grid their influence in relation to the birth date can be interpreted easily.

FIXED GRID

3	6	9
2	5	8
1	4	7

BIRTH GRID

		9
1 0	4 4 4	

NAME GRID

3	2	3
1	5	1
5	1	1

The mental plane, which is blank in the birth date, except for the century 9, has been greatly strengthened. The emotional plane has been helped by the 5 vibration. Positivity has been introduced by the 1 vibration on the physical plane.

Most importantly, the name Caroline vibrates to the number 5 which alleviates the drabness of the 4 vibration controlling the personality.

More information on this part of our analysis is given in Chapter 10, The Significance of the Letters of the Whole Name.

The analysis of the numbers of the birth date is now complete. These first two Spheres of Influence have the strongest bearing on the formation and development of our personalities.

We are fortunate if all, or most of the vibrations of our birth date, combine in harmony and we can find specific direction easily. However, if the vibrationary influences are in conflict, the challenge we face is how best to manage the divergent influences pushing us in inconsistent directions. In many cases, self-discipline and sheer willpower can contain the effect of contrary and negative tendencies. But other personalities may need some assistance. This assistance may be provided by the name.

If the name is ineffective or emphasises weaknesses rather than giving strength and balance, it may be beneficial to modify the name to produce the influences that will do so.

In order to appreciate how a name can change aspects of personality, its role in shaping character and destiny must first be analysed. The Third, Fourth, Fifth and Sixth Spheres of Influence reveal how this is done.

THE THIRD SPHERE OF INFLUENCE
THE GIVEN NAME

The vibrations of the name contribute to the Third, Fourth, Fifth and Sixth Spheres of Influence. The given name as the Third Sphere of Influence has a significant role in balancing the vibrations of the Birth Grid, as seen in the examples at the end of this chapter. If areas of conflict appear in the birth date, the vibration of the Third Sphere could neutralise the conflict, but it may also strengthen the problem. Our aim is to encourage people to use given names in a way that will enhance the birth date and help create more balanced individuals who would therefore be better prepared to fulfil their potential.

While the given name has the most important role of a name, the vibrations of the middle name, or names (if any) and the surname all add to the composite of a personality. The surname reflects hereditary tendencies and family resemblances. It is only in these areas that it has any significance. The middle name or names form the passive part and do not possess an independent function but contribute to the formation of the full name and the compound number of the full name. This contribution could be valuable when the given name and surname are both short, such as "Ann Hill, or "Ian Hall". The letters, and correspondingly the numbers, of these names are so few that the supply of vibrations to the overall personality is meagre.

A strong and balanced birth date will be needed to get by without supporting vibrations from the names. When the numbers of the names are listed and compared with the grid of the birth date, the desirability of at least one middle name will become apparent. More information on this aspect of the complete chart is given in Chapter 10.

"What's in a name?" is a question we hear from time to time. Shakespeare himself asked this question and added that "a rose by any other name would smell as sweet". Irrespective of the context in which this question is asked, it will be our endeavour to show that there is a great deal of significance in a name and that the giving of any name — one that is constantly used — is indeed a matter worth serious consideration.

The given name may have been the decision of parents, ourselves, or others. Often a middle name or some other name unrelated to those on the birth certificate may be in use. It is this name which identifies and gives individuality and which has the most significant effect on the personality. For instance, a child christened or named Percival Edward Smith may sooner or later prefer his middle name, Edward, which in turn may be changed to Ted. Therefore, as far as this work is concerned, his given name is Ted.

When a given name is chosen we need to take into consideration the common practice of multi-syllabled names being abbreviated or altered. If this new version is kept in permanent use it will be the one that holds the power of sound and influence. For example, if the name Genevieve is chosen for its 7 vibration, the girl will probably lose it to the 11 which is Genny or the 5 which is Jenny. Similarly, James may become Jim (5), Jimmy (7) or Jamie (2). There is something to be said for parents insisting that children are called by the name they know is best.

Some people may always be referred to or addressed by their initials or titles, or by double or even treble names. Some examples are "G.B.S", Boss, Chief, Oscar Wilde, Mary Grant Bruce. There are others who have two sets of names, one used in business and another within the family and by intimate friends. In the first example the total of the initials or the total of the multiple names is the number to consider. For people who use two sets of names the vibrations produced by both names are equally important and should be examined to see whether they are in harmony with the particular area of activity they are influencing. Nicknames and pet names possess the same power and influence as the given name. People who have these extra names will have two or more vibrations influencing them.

A name is, in fact, a sound. The power of the given name is generated from the vibrations of sound and sound waves beyond the reach of human hearing. A better appreciation of the power of the given name will be gained if both the general constructive power of sound and the destructive power of sound vibrations are understood. Students of Cosmogony are aware that it was the sound vibrations of the Word of the Creator that brought all creation into being. The therapeutic value of music, particularly the chant, is well recognised. A branch of Yoga known as Mantra Yoga is confined to the vibrations of sound.

The human body with its psyche is a finely tuned instrument with keen responses to all sorts of extraneous vibrations, particularly the vibrations of sound. There is an instant feeling of well-being when a sympathetic vibration is encountered and displeasure with an inharmonious vibration. As all bodies are of different rates of vibration they do not respond in the same way to the same vibration, whether sound or otherwise. Herein lies the reason for the importance of the choice of a given name which needs to be in harmony with a particular type of body and personality. An inharmonious name will be like a discordant musical note causing discomfort, restriction and imbalance. This point is well illustrated by William Congreve in the following lines:

Music hath charms to soothe a savage breast,
To soften rocks, or bend a knotted oak.
I've read that things inanimate have moved,
And, as with living souls, have been informed
By magic numbers and persuasive sound.

As a further illustration we shall use the name Leanne. Leanne is addressed several times a day by different people who have a mental picture of her personality. Each time the name is used the sound vibrations of the word "Leanne" created in the speaker's voice box issue forth in wave formation and merge with the vibratory complex that is Leanne and at the same time are broadcast for all around to hear and feel. Not only is there a merging of these vibrations with Leanne's physical body and personality but there is also a bouncing off or dispersion of these vibrations around her, creating a sort of aura. This is a constant battering process which goes on throughout Leanne's life. She is in fact brought into the direct firing line of the mental vibration 6 which is the number of Leanne. The vibratory qualities of this number thrust at her repeatedly are absorbed as part of her individuality and cause her to react unconsciously and to adopt the particular traits of this number, and this is often seen and interpreted by others as her personality. Though Leanne may be seen by others through the vibrations of her name, her real personality could be much more complex.

If Leanne's birth date is 3.6.1923=24=6, hers will be an unsuitable name, for she is by birth already a mentally oriented person with great need for stability on the physical plane. She has no need for more mental vibrations which can only produce a lopsided or top-heavy personality. She would be better off with a name adding up to the physical vibrations 1, 4 or 7, preferably in that order. On the other hand, if Leanne was born on 1 . 7 . 1957 = 30 = 3, she would have an ideal name, providing balance to her personality and assisting her destiny since the numbers 6 and 3 are in harmony. The many qualities associated with domesticity will also be contributed.

The classical name "Jason" has been in vogue in recent times. The vibration of this name is 5 and it would be a splendid name for a bright lad born on 3.11.1973 = 25 = 7. The emotional plane in this birth date is blank, but the 5 name of Jason will see that this individual will have no problems in functioning on all planes of activity. The vital connecting link of the 5 vibration will form a fine balance within the personality. This name, however, will not be suitable for a boy born on, say, 5.2.1955=27=9. Hyperactivity and excess of emotion, among other difficulties, will be the result of overloading the 5 vibration.

Care should therefore be taken to choose a given name that fits into the grid of the birth date, either giving balance to the personality in an area that is blank, or giving strength to an area that has a number but needs strengthening.

Whenever possible, preference should be given to 1 names or 5 names, for these are the true activators. In a well-distributed birth date, such as 23 . 6 . 1964 = 31 = 4, a 1 name will be most advantageous because it will give strength and self-confidence to a multi-talented personality. The weak century 1, which we all possess, does not produce these qualities.

As the 5 vibration is the communicator with all the other numbers, a 5 name will be ideal if the middle horizontal area or the middle vertical area, or both, are blank. The grid of Jason's first birth date clearly shows this need.

3 3	9
1 1 1	7 7

Note: The First Sphere of Influence is underlined once. The Second Sphere of Influence is underlined twice.

If a birth date is found to be strong as well as balanced and no help is needed from the given name, the best choice will be a name that will be in harmony with the destiny number. The question of overloading does not arise since the Spheres of Influence are different. A birth date such as 18 . 3 . 1954 = 31 = 4 does not need help from the given name to strengthen the personality. A 4 name will be best so that added help is given towards fulfilling the 4 destiny.

The point to be remembered is that the given name influences the personality and therefore shares common ground with the First Sphere of Influence which forms the personality. The vibrations of the given name should not clash with, weaken, or disturb the vibrations of the First Sphere of Influence. The repetition of a vibration in the same sphere or on the same plane is the quickest way to activate negative aspects of numbers. For instance, a birth date such as 8 . 8 . 1938 should not have an 8 given name and a 3 name will be most unsuitable for someone born on 3 . 3 . 1983.

Parents choose names for their children from many sources. Names of family members are often repeated in the next generation, names are borrowed from well-known identities, "pop-names" in current vogue spread rapidly, or parents can express their creativity with a unique name or unusual spelling. While these names may please the parents, the children are not always grateful and in fact may feel handicapped.

Though Dad may feel proud that he has passed the name Maxwell on to his son, and Aunt Agatha is happy that her niece will carry on her name, the children may feel quite the opposite. Names that are obviously dated at the time of naming can be an embarrassment to the children and they may also create the wrong vibrations. Boys have been named "Conan" after the aggressive character in the film *Conan the Barbarian*, while internationally acclaimed pop songs inspired "Roxanne" and "Rhiannon" — but Roxanne was a prostitute and Rhiannon a witch. Though these names may have appealed to the parents, the children may have to live with numerological vibrations that cause conflict and connotations that could lead to the use of unpleasant nicknames.

This blindfolded, hit-or-miss method of giving names is unnecessary, for any concerned person may choose a name from among hundreds that will be in harmony and balance with the birth date. In doing so they will make a significant contribution towards the development of a well-balanced individual. The idea is that the name chosen should not only be pleasing to the parents but should also be one that will relate favourably to the personality and destiny of the child.

The final choice of the name should be made after many alternatives have been examined, not only for their direct influence on the personality but also for their very significant contribution to the formation of the three other Spheres of Influence, especially the compound number of the full name. In a weak birth date a name can be chosen that will produce a strong digit in the Fourth Sphere of Influence and will give support and strength to the personality.

The names listed in this book have all been numerically calculated and classified according to their Third Sphere vibration. This number is produced by adding together all the numerical values of each letter in the name and reducing the total to a single digit. The names that carry Master vibrations are shown under 11 and 22 as well as under their single-digit values of 2 and 4.

To use these name lists to their full advantage it is best to plot the birth dates or predicted birth dates on grids, as described in Chapter 5. Parents may then use the knowledge accumulated from the previous chapters to determine which numbers would provide the benefits needed by the birth date or birth dates. Once it has been established which numbers are required, a short list of names may be chosen to correspond with these numbers.

It is important for parents to remain flexible about a name for their baby. They should consider each name carefully and concentrate on the name that they feel sounds best, or feels "right".

Numerologists believe that parents are not the only ones to have a bearing on the choice of the name for their children; higher forces also influence the decision. Though parents may systematically analyse the factors described in this book and narrow down the list of prospective names, they should try not to be dominated by this "mental" perspective but should also try to let intuition play a part.

CHANGING THE GIVEN NAME

Choosing a name for a baby means that we can start with a fresh slate and work with the prospective birth date to choose a name that it will be beneficial to the child. But as adults we already have a name and need to work with it in the first instance to produce harmony within the personality and a lifestyle that is successful. A complete change of name is necessary only in special circumstances. An adult should first try changing the spelling of their name, if a change is considered necessary.

It may sound far-fetched but it has been proved that a change of name will in most instances slowly but surely cause a corresponding change in the personality, or an intensification of certain characteristics of the personality. Sometimes the change is quite sudden. The length of time it takes to notice a change will no doubt depend on the purpose of the change and the potential already present to respond to the new vibration. Generally, an instant change should not be expected.

The vibrations of the new name will take time to influence the personality, depending on the degree of conscious identification with the new vibration or the lifting of the whole personality to catch the full power of the new vibration. This process might take three months or three years, depending on the individual.

Existing potential is essential before a new name can trigger off a change of career or cause a career to escalate. If a name is changed for this purpose, as in the case of many artists, actors and people entering religious orders, the vibration of the new name should not only fit and harmonise with the Second Sphere of Influence (Destiny) and the Fourth Sphere of Influence (Expression of Talents) but also with the particular career chosen. In other words, the sound of the new name must be pleasant and appropriate to the career intended. Innumerable actors who have found their original names a liability have achieved success and fame by adopting pleasant sounding names of compatible vibrations.

Changing names to suit vocations and new vocations, especially in religious orders, has been a common practice all over the world for centuries. Both the Old and New Testaments of the Bible are replete with instances of names being deliberately changed before a specific vocation or mission was undertaken.

Many people also change their name for the purpose of bringing about balance and harmony within the personality, with no other motive in mind, though their real reason for doing so, being personal, is not often revealed.

Although the idea of changing one's name may sound attractive and desirable at times, it is not a step to be taken without serious consideration and consultation if necessary.

Many questions should be asked and answered before a decision is made, such as:

(a) Is a change really necessary?

(b) Have the birth and name grids been examined properly?

(c) What are the motives for the change? Are they for frivolous reasons, or are escapist tendencies involved? Often it is better to retain the name and overcome any obstacles, real or imagined, that it may cause. Students of the inner side of things understand that for the most part our names have been given to us for a purpose.

(d) Has advice been sought and considered? A wrong choice may lead to many disturbances within the personality and these would adversely affect the career and personal relations.

(e) Has a change of spelling of the present name been considered? This is often the best alternative. The same pronunciation can be retained by adding, removing or changing a letter or letters. The change in spelling of the name alters its rate of vibration and correspondingly the influence upon the personality. We should keep in mind that it is the most suitable vibration we are seeking and not merely a new name that happens to be currently popular.

If any doubts linger after the suggestions in this book have been considered, a numerologist's opinion may be sought. The final choice of a name, however, always rests with the parents or the individual. A third party should only give an opinion.

$$23 . 4 . 1967 = 32 = 5$$

3	6	9
2	5 5	
1	4	7

Note: The First Sphere of Influence is underlined once. The Second Sphere of Influence is underlined twice.

Comments: Multi-talented and well balanced but lacking in drive as a result of the absence of a strong 1 vibration. A 1 name is essential for self-confidence.

$$31 . 5 . 1972 = 28 = 10 = 1$$

3		9
2	5	
1 1 <u>1</u>	<u>4</u>	7

Comments: Stong, well balanced and multi-talented. Assistance from the name is not called for, but a 6 name, giving domesticity, would be good.

$$1 . 4 . 1940 = 19 = 10 = 1$$

		9
0 1 <u>1</u> <u>1</u>	4 4	

Comments: Physically oriented. A 5 name should be chosen for flexibility, imagination, and oral and emotional expression. Names with physical plane numbers will increase rigidity.

$$20 . 2 . 1958 = 27 = 9$$

		9 <u>9</u>
2 <u>2</u>	5	8
0 1		

Comments: Emotionally overbalanced. A 1 name is essential to reduce emotionalism and provide some stability in the physical plane. A 4 or 7 name could be a second choice. Names with emotional plane numbers should not be considered.

$$3 . 9 . 1935 = 30 = 3$$

3 3 3		9 9
	5	
1		

Comments: Mentally overbalanced. A 4 name would be best to bring this personality down to earth. 1 and 7 names would be good alternatives. Names with mental plane numbers would threaten mental stability.

$$12 . 1 . 1931 = 18 = 9$$

3 3		9 9
2		
1 1 1 1		

Comments: Egocentric. A 5 name would help the personality to cross over central blanks and help fulfil the wide-ranging 9 destiny. 1 and 3 names should be avoided.

$$7 . 7 . 1977 = 38 = 11$$

		9
(11)1		7777

Comments: Introverted and pedantic. A 5 name would open out the personality. 2 and 3 names would be good alternatives and would soften rigid attitudes. A 7 name would be disastrous.

$$5 . 1 . 1988 = 32 = 5$$

		9
	5 5	8 8
1 1		

Comments: As the 5 vibration controls both the First and Second Spheres of Influence, excess of speed and excessive expenditure of nervous energy could be a problem. A 4, 6 or 7 name would slow down the personality. A 5 name would cause excessive tension and hyperactivity.

$$21 . 2 . 1997 = 31 = 4$$

3		9 9
2 2		
1 1	4	7

Comments: A versatile personality with positive attitudes. A 6 or 4 name would assist Destiny and add a link to the second vertical area of the grid. A 5 name will bring in too much emotion.

$$5 . 5 . 2000 = 12 = 3$$

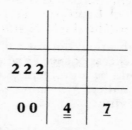

Comments: Extreme restlessness and instability will be shown by this negative Five personality with a Three Destiny. A name with another mental or emotional number would aggravate these problems. A name with a physical plane number is essential.

$$7 . 2 . 2002 = 13 = 4$$

Comments: Introversion will be a problem here. A 3 name will open out the personality. A 5 name would be a good alternative.

THE FOURTH SPHERE OF INFLUENCE
THE WHOLE NAME

The Fourth Sphere of Influence lies within the single digit arrived at from the summation of the numerical value of the letters of the whole name. It indicates, on the one hand, the talents with which we are endowed and, on the other hand, it serves as a channel for these talents to be expressed. This sphere is also known as the Sphere of Expression and should be examined when choosing a career. The single digit needed is arrived at as follows:

P	E	R	C	I	V	A	L		E	D	W	A	R	D		S	M	I	T	H
7	5	9	3	9	4	1	3		5	4	5	1	9	4		1	4	9	2	8

$$41 \qquad\qquad 28 \qquad\qquad 24$$
$$5 \qquad\qquad 10 \qquad\qquad 6$$
$$5 \quad + \quad 1 \quad + \quad 6 = 12 = 3$$

We suggest that the single digit of each name is recorded as above and the three (or more) single digits are added together to ascertain the final number. By doing this, the manner in which the final number is formed will be observed.

In our example, a 5 given name, a 1 middle name and a 6 surname have produced a composite number of 12, reducing to the final digit 3. This final digit is the summation of the qualities of all the individual letters of the three names. These details will be helpful when examining two or more people with the same final digit number in their whole name but who express themselves with some differences. These differences are the result of the fact that their composite numbers are formed differently and therefore possess inherent variations. For example, an individual with a final digit of 3, formed as in the name Percival Smith, will express his or her personality and talents with some differences to one whose final digit is formed from a 9 given name, a 4 middle name and an 8 surname which adds up to 21 = 3.

It may be considered fortunate if the talents an individual already possesses, which are indicated and expressed by this Fourth Sphere, are found to complement the Second Sphere of Influence (Destiny). The position will be even better if the personality type (First Sphere) is also supportive. The fulfilment of Destiny will then be made so much easier. A harmonious combination of these important spheres of influence will provide considerable support to the vocations and hobbies to be followed.

Hobbies and recreational activities should be considered seriously since they provide diversification of interests. Not infrequently, an avocation takes over from the vocation and becomes the source of fame and fortune. Meanwhile, hobbies and interests could provide personal fulfilment which may not be found in regular employment. They may also provide incentive for early retirement and the avenue for developing new interests in life.

There is little doubt that the First, Second and Fourth Spheres of Influence need to work together for success and balance. However, if these spheres are on different planes of expression, they need not be allowed to pull the personality in opposite directions but may be used to extend the talents and widen the range of expression of the personality. The three spheres clamouring for attention and motivation at the same time should be recognised and reconciled. As an example we may consider Percival Smith's Fourth Sphere of Influence in relation to his birth date, which is 20 . 12 . 1938 = 26 = 8.

A cursory glance at his 8 Destiny (Second Sphere) and his 3 talents (Fourth Sphere) may indicate that they are basically opposed to each other — the businesslike 8 and the lighthearted 3. But a closer examination will reveal that his Two personality (First Sphere) and his talents show many shared characteristics and others that can work in harmony. His social and artistic expression is very strong. He will display exceptional ability as a Public Relations Officer. If these talents are combined and used in the Second Sphere of Destiny in businesses connected with entertainment, success is assured. The leadership of the 3 and the diplomacy of the 2 can combine with the organisation and method of the 8. The idea is to recognise and extract the best qualities of each sphere and use them as a potentially successful team.

What follows is a comprehensive list of occupations relative to each number. As certain vibrations share common characteristics, though expressed differently, people influenced by sympathetic vibrations are attracted to similar types of occupations. As such, generalisation is necessarily the basis in presenting a list of this nature. The occupations given under each number are the ones in which fulfilment and success will be achieved naturally and easily. It will also be observed after a close look at all the numbers that some occupations just do not attract people of certain vibrations.

This occupation list can help steer us in the direction in which our natural talents lie. It can be of particular help to parents, students and people seeking employment or change of employment.

Adults who are already in employment and feel content with their jobs and know they do them well will probably find their occupations listed under the numbers of their First, Second or Fourth Spheres of Influence. They may also find that many jobs they have seriously considered are listed.

Those who do not enjoy their jobs and often feel as if they are square pegs in round holes, may look closely at the jobs listed under the numbers of their First, Second and Fourth Spheres of Influence. They may quite possibly see avenues of employment they have desired and hobbies they have fancied.

We should remember that while the Fourth Sphere's main purpose is to influence our choice of occupation (paid or recreational) by providing us with certain talents, the directions pointed out by our Destiny should be our first consideration. Our second consideration should be the best combination of talents we can get together from the First and Fourth Spheres of Influence, not forgetting advantages we may have in the Sixth Sphere (outer person).

VIBRATION NUMBER 1 — OCCUPATION

Apiarists
Architects
Assayers
Bushwalkers
Composers of music
Conductors and leaders of
    orchestras
Designers
Detectives
Drovers

Editors
Engineers
Entrepreneurs
Estate agents
Excavators
Executives
Explorers
Farmers
Glassblowers
Graziers
Inventors
Managers
Manufacturers
Merchant seamen

Metallurgists
Overseers
Pioneers
Playwrights
Politicians
Producers
Printers
Publishers
Research scientists
Sports professionals
Tailors
Taxi drivers
Weavers
Wine producers

VIBRATION NUMBER 2 — OCCUPATION

Actors (*romance*)
Advertisers
Ambulance officers
Arbitrators
Bacteriologists
Ballet dancers and teachers
Beauticians
Biographers
Bookbinders
Bus drivers
Butlers
Calligraphers
Childcare workers
Clerks
Collectors
Companions
Computer programmers
Correspondents
Credit officers
Curators (*art galleries and museums*)
Dancers and dancing instructors
Deputies
Diplomats
Domestic servants
Dressmakers

Embroiderers
Engineers (*electronics*)
Engravers
Entertainers (*in groups*)
Florists
Genealogists
Glassblowers
Goldsmiths
Hairdressers
Historians
Homemakers
Hosts and hostesses
Ice skaters
Librarians
Mediators
Medical practitioners
Meteorologists
Musicians
Nurses
Opticians
Pastry cooks
Pawnbrokers
Personnel officers
Photographers
Process workers
Psychics
Secretaries

Shoemakers
Signwriters
Silversmiths
Social workers
Spiritual healers
Statisticians
Striptease artists

Taxi drivers
Tour directors
Truck drivers
Travel agents
Waiters
Watchmakers
Writers (*romance*)

VIBRATION NUMBER 3 — OCCUPATION

Accountants
Actors (*comedians*)
Advertisers
Announcers
Art critics
Art dealers
Artists
Beauticians
Cabaret artists
Cabinet makers
Callers
Cartoonists
Choreographers
Commentators
Comperes
Cosmetics manufacturers
Decorators
Designers (*clothes*)
Disc jockeys
Editors (*social*)
Entertainers (*solo*)
Executives
Fashion models

Goldsmiths
Hairdressers
Hosts and hostesses
Inventors
Instructors
Jewellers
Journalists
Lawyers
Lecturers
Managers
Military officers
Ministers of religion
Musicians
Poets
Politicians
Printers
Salespersons
Signwriters
Scouts and guides
Social secretaries
Window dressers
Writers (*short stories*)

VIBRATION NUMBER 4 — OCCUPATION

Accountants
Agriculturalists
Appraisers
Archaeologists
Assayers
Auditors
Bookbinders
Bookkeepers

Business proprietors
Buyers
Cabinet makers
Carpenters
Cartoonists
Clerks
Clothiers
Concretors

Credit officers
Dentists
Draftspeople
Economists
Efficiency experts
Engineers (*construction*)
Estimators
Excavators
Farmers
Fire officers
Geologists
Graziers
Guards (*security*)
Hardware merchants
Horticulturalists
Joiners
Labourers
Masons
Masseurs
Mechanics
Metallurgists

Miners
Musicians (*drums and martial music*)
Pawnbrokers
Plumbers
Police officers
Potters
Process workers
Professionals in sport
Protocol officers
Real estate agents
Sculptors
Signwriters
Soldiers
Statisticians
Storekeepers
Surgeons
Technicians
Undertakers
Valuers

VIBRATION NUMBER 5 — OCCUPATION

Acrobats
Actors (*drama*)
Administrators
Advertisers
Ambulance officers
Bartenders
Broadcasters
Bus drivers
Cabaret artists
Chauffeurs
Circus performers (*including clowns*)
Coaches (*sport*)
Commercial travellers
Comperes
Critics
Couriers
Demonstrators
Detectives
Disc jockeys
Drovers

Editors
Electrical engineers
Entrepreneurs (*sport and entertainment*)
Explorers
Fashion models
Fire officers
Freedom fighters
Gamblers (*professional*)
Humorists
Interpreters
Investigators
Journalists (*freelance*)
Lawyers
Lecturers
Linguists
Lobbyists
Military officers
Mountaineers
Organisers
Personnel managers

Photographers
Police officers
Politicians
Promoters
Psychologists
Publishers
Racing car drivers
Salespersons
Spies
Taxi drivers

Test pilots
Tour guides
Translators
Travellers
Unionists
Volunteer workers (*specialised or dangerous work*)
Welfare workers
Writers (*controversial issues*)

VIBRATION NUMBER *6* — OCCUPATION

Actors (*drama*)
Bakers
Bartenders
Butlers
Caretakers
Caterers (*food*)
Chefs
Chauffeurs
Childcare workers
Connoisseurs (*food, wine, fine arts*)
Cooks
Counsellors
Dancing teachers
Decorators
Diplomats
Domestic service (*butlers and governesses*)
Drapers
Drink waiters
Florists
Girl Guides leaders
Historians
Homemakers
Hosts and hostesses (*entertainment and hospitality industries*)

Hotel executives (*in motels, apartment houses, homes for the aged; in businesses dealing with food, household requirements, clothing, cosmetics, perfumes and educational supplies*)
Innkeepers
Lawyers
Lecturers
Lobbyists
Marriage celebrants
Masseurs
Medical practitioners
Mimics
Personnel officers
Philosophers
Poets
Restaurateurs
Scoutmasters
Social workers
Song writers
Storytellers
Teachers
Waiters (*food and drink*)
Welfare workers
Wine tasters

VIBRATION NUMBER *7* — OCCUPATION

Accountants
Anthropologists

Antique dealers and collectors
Apiarists

Archaeologists
Archivists
Astrologers
Astronomers
Artists (*landscape*)
Bacteriologists
Bankers
Biologists
Brewers
Brokers
Canoeists
Chemists
Composers of music
Curators (*museums*)
Drovers
Excavators
Farmers
Finance brokers
Financiers
Fishermen
Florists
Forest rangers
Gardeners
Geographers
Geologists
Greengrocers
Graziers
Historians (*Ancient History*)
Horticulturalists
Inventors
Investigators

Investors
Laboratory workers
Lawyers
Lecturers
Lighthouse keepers
Market gardeners
Medical specialists
Meteorologists
Miners
Ministers of religion
Naturalists
Nurserymen
Palaeontologists
Pharmacists
Poets
Poultry farmers
Private investigators
Professors
Psychiatrists
Psychoanalysts
Quality controllers
Real estate agents
Research workers
Secret service agents
Scientists (*space age*)
Statisticians
Wine producers
Writers (*science, philosophy, mystery*)
Zoologists

VIBRATION NUMBER 8 — OCCUPATION

Accountants
Administrators
Bankers
Brokers
Builders
Bureaucrats
Business people
Buyers
Coaches (*sport*)
Computer programmers

Contractors
Efficiency experts
Executives
Financial counsellors
Financiers
Funeral directors
Insurance (*all types*)
Judges
Legislators
Managers

Manufacturers
Organisers
Politicians
Ship builders

Sports professionals
Town planners
Treasurers
Union officials

VIBRATION NUMBER **9** — *OCCUPATION*

Academics
Actors (*tragedians*)
Administrators
Artists
Bacteriologists
Bus and coach drivers
Bushwalkers
Comperes
Composers of music
Conductors of orchestras
Curators (*museums and art galleries*)
Dancers and dancing instructors
Decorators
Diagnosticians
Dieticians
Diplomats
Editors

Fashion Models
Horticulturalists
Journalists
Ministers of religion
Medicine (*all branches*)
Missionaries
Musicians
Novelists
Organists
Philosophers
Poets
Poultry breeders
Printers
Restorers of art works
Singers
Spiritual healers
Teachers
Travellers

VIBRATION NUMBER **11** — *OCCUPATION*

Actors
Advertisers
Announcers
Astrologers
Astronomers
Comperes
Composers of music
Dressmakers
Engineers (*electronics*)
Evangelists
Explorers (*scientific and metaphysical*)
Inventors
Lobbyists

Mediums
Meteorologists
Missionaries
Orators
Philosophers
Politicians
Psychics
Psychoanalysts
Psychologists
Publishers
Reformers
Radio and television technicians
Salespersons

Scientists (*space*)   Writers (*inspirational and
Song writers   scientific*)

VIBRATION NUMBER 22 — OCCUPATION

Subjects of this Master vibration may choose any field of human endeavour and be assured of leaving their footprints behind. It is the one vibration that contains the characteristics of all others and gives its subjects the power to function with equal ease on the physical, emotional, mental and inspirational planes.

THE FIFTH SPHERE OF INFLUENCE
VOWELS OF THE WHOLE NAME

Among the vowels of the whole name may be found the heart of a person, or to put it another way, the most subtle aspects of the personality. As there is certainly a concealment here, this Fifth Sphere of Influence is usually referred to as the inner person. It is the sphere of inner desires usually familiar only to the individual. It may also be described as the fundamental stratum or bedrock of the personality that is not displayed to others and therefore rarely known, except to those fortunate or unfortunate ones, as the case may be, who have had many opportunities over a period of time to penetrate beyond the facade into the depths of the personality.

The concealment we find here makes the Fifth Sphere the least apparent but it is no less significant than the others. In fact, it takes precedence over the others at certain times during the life span of the great majority of people. Anything that lies hidden tends to arouse curiosity and anticipation. Hence, the disclosure of the nature of this Sphere of Influence always provides surprises. It is an area of the personality closely associated with the subconscious mind representing inner urges, promptings, desires and longings, and is not to be taken as representing outer personality traits, accomplishments or requirements. The forces within this sphere, however, constantly seek outlets, and to the degree that these outlets are found and used, a roundness of the personality is achieved. If no opening is found in any one or more of the other Spheres of Influence the personality may suffer from disillusionment and frustration until, through self-study, the situation is recognised and personal adjustments are made.

Despite the fact that this is generally a concealed area there are instances where people "wear their hearts on their sleeves". These are the open personalities that are sometimes encountered. There is usually a variation in the degree of influence of the forces of this sphere. They could be dormant, ignored or suppressed, or consciously and intelligently used and in some instances become extremely active or suddenly awakened. A sudden inexplicable change in a seemingly established lifestyle may be the result of an abrupt awakening of the inner forces, which have found a ready outlet for active participation with the other Spheres of Influence.

The Fifth Sphere assumes considerable importance when undertaking a permanent or long-term partnership of any sort, for whatever facade or feigned condition a person may assume temporarily in order to achieve a particular objective, that person will sooner or later revert to fundamental desires.

Partners in marriage should ascertain and understand the nature of each other's inner persons for the success of the partnership. For instance, if the Fifth Sphere of one partner is influenced by the 7 vibration, which yearns for tranquillity, silence and abstract study, and if in the other this sphere is influenced by the outgoing 3 vibration, there will be problems sooner or later, unless there has been a process of sorting out, understanding and adjustment.

In order to ascertain the secrets of this intriguing sphere, the usual practice of converting the letters of the whole name to their numerical values is followed, but for this purpose the vowels only are used. After conversion they are added together and the compound number reduced to a single digit as in the following example:

P E R C I V A L   E D W A R D   S M I T H

$$5 \quad 9 \quad 1 \quad 5 \quad \quad 1 \quad \quad \quad 9$$
$$15 \quad\quad\quad\quad 6 \quad\quad\quad\quad 9$$
$$6 \quad\quad + \quad\quad 6 \quad\quad + \quad\quad 9 = 21 = 3$$

The inner person of our fictitious Mr Smith will radiate from the depths of his personality the qualities of the 3 vibration in the distinctive way they emerge through this particular Sphere of Influence. The Master numbers 11 and 22 operate in this sphere as well and therefore should not be reduced further.

The vowels A, E, I, O and U are converted directly to 1, 5, 9, 6 and 3 respectively. The letter Y, converting to 7, is counted as a vowel if it is found in a position where it functions as a vowel, as in the following instances:

(a) When there is no other vowel in the name, as in Flynn or Lynn.
(b) When there is no vowel in the syllable, as in Tyrone or Sylvia.
(c) When it is preceded by another vowel and sounded as one, as in Guy or Jayne.

VIBRATION NUMBER 1
Inner Person

The 1 vibration is experienced as a constant pressure on the ego to assume the general characteristics of this vibration, especially those of independence and leadership. People with this number as their inner urge will automatically take over and direct any situation in which they may find themselves. They will find personal satisfaction only when they are giving orders and not when they are taking them. If not in a position of authority they prefer to work on their own, unhampered by interference and restrictions.

The degree to which this inner compulsion is achieved will depend on the compatibility between this vibration and those in the other Spheres of Influence. If there is an opening in any one or more of the other Spheres of Influence, particularly in the First Sphere, these individuals will be capable of considerable accomplishment. Their strong inner drive will carry them through any rough patches in their lives and in the lives of those associated with them, much to the surprise of people who are unaware of this inner strength. This trait is often revealed not only in their personal lives but also in times of civil disorder and warfare.

The creative forces of this vibration constantly seek means of fulfilment, and in instances where outlets may not exist for leadership of people, these creative forces may still provide many satisfying avenues for self-fulfilment. The creativity of One personalities will lead them into entrepreneurial activities and careers in fashion designing. They will always be in the forefront in business and social life.

In personal relationships they will reveal sooner or later many unsuspected qualities such as loyalty, willpower, ambition, authority and pride. The negative personalities will be conceited, critical, dictatorial and selfish.

VIBRATION NUMBER 2
Inner Person

Companionship, accompanied by love, kindliness, peace and harmony, will be the strongest yearning of people with the 2 vibration in the Fifth Sphere. There will be no inner incitement towards competition, ambition, commercialism and popularity through wealth and power. They will seek to cooperate, assist, support and serve. They will often withdraw into the 2 vibration's characteristic pastime of fantasy. The positive Twos will find real enjoyment in their beautiful mental creations, while the negative ones will indulge in pessimistic and melancholy thoughts.

Their strong psychic sense constantly seeks to surface itself but may easily be stifled by environmental influences or by other areas of the personality that may be antagonistic or indifferent to psychic manifestation and development. The real inner strength of these personalities lies in their qualities of compassion, understanding, diplomacy, flexibility and generosity on the one hand, and the absence of greed, jealousy, pride, anger and resentment on the other. Weaknesses such as a lack of willpower and self-discipline, indecisiveness and excessive diffidence will be common in the more negative personalities.

VIBRATION NUMBER 3
Inner Person

The driving forces behind this vibration of youth, such as the need for self-expression, the desire for popularity and the zest for living, all seek outlets. These people are dreamers at heart and their vivid imaginations impel them to seek various means by which their mental creations may be expressed. Oral expression takes first place. The desire to speak out, to give orders, express opinions and to entertain will be irresistible. Their sense of beauty, colour, creative impulses and emotion constantly seek avenues of expression.

A close relationship with these people will soon reveal generous, joyful, optimistic and entertaining personalities without the debilitating influences of worry, depression and melancholy. Their strength and weakness both lie in their great need, not only for social intercourse, but also to occupy the centre position in any social gathering. The positive ones have no difficulty in achieving these desires. The negative ones usually resort to creating situations, usually unpleasant, whereby they become the centre of attention.

They will never want to lag behind or fall into a rut. Attempts to suppress or hold back these people will not succeed in the long run because of the constant demand within themselves to keep abreast of current happenings and to play an active part. Unless supported by other vibrations they will not be happy if confined entirely to a domestic scene or forced into routine, detail and monotony. If regular work does not include productive activity their inner urges for artistic creation, social involvement and expression of emotion will be satisfied by interests outside their normal responsibilities.

VIBRATION NUMBER 4
Inner Person

The enduring qualities of dependability, honesty, loyalty and service — to family, community and country — form the bedrock of all people with this vibration controlling the Fifth Sphere of Influence. Any attempt to enlist them to rebel against, or question, traditional ways of life will be firmly rebuffed. They are entirely at ease accepting and upholding the established laws and customs of the land. When committed to or enlisted in a cause, their self-discipline and self-sacrifice will soon be revealed, much to the relief of those depending on them. They are followers rather than leaders and are unlikely to question authority.

They are unable to enjoy relaxation and ease if a job remains to be done or has not been completed. Full inner contentment is achieved when all responsibilities have been attended to in their usual efficient manner. Lack of a lively imagination and resentment of change may finally disclose serious and sedate personalities, especially in personal relationships, when some gaiety, frivolity and humour is expected. This is amply compensated, however, by the sincerity, security and stability they provide in any relationship.

Family love and family pride are fundamental to these people, who will resist with great vehemence any assaults on the security and good name of the family. Their love is deep and ironclad though not demonstrated by a great show of emotion. Laziness and dullness will override the mentality of negative people with the 4 vibration in this Sphere.

VIBRATION NUMBER 5
Inner Person

The heart's desire of the 5 vibration is freedom of expression, which is its principal motivating force, and the need for a diversified lifestyle becomes an integral part of this freedom. Considerable disturbance within the personality will result if opportunities for freedom of expression are not available through the other Spheres of Influence and in the environment in which they live. The curiosity of the 5 vibration, which is now at the foundation of the personality, must also be satisfied. If not, these people will use both straightforward and devious methods to do so.

Impatience stirs them into action. This inner restlessness must be understood and recognised by the individuals themselves, and by others, and adjustment to their lifestyle made accordingly. It must be known that deep within these people lie intelligent, alert, quick-witted and volatile personalities. Opportunities to indulge in variety should be available, especially to children, so that expansion of the inner person is not stifled.

It may not always be possible to comply with the yearning for travel, which is always present wherever the 5 vibration operates. However, this can be satisfied by a variety of literature and a vocation or avocation as a writer. The written word can be made the channel by which the courage, restlessness and other outward characteristics of this vibration can be expressed. Many successful freelance correspondents are subjects of this vibration.

In personal relationships it must be recognised that the 5 is not a domestic number and those influenced by it in any of the Spheres of Influence should not be committed entirely to such responsibilities because very little success and much failure will be the result.

VIBRATION NUMBER 6
Inner Person

The 6 vibration will exercise a firm grip on the domestic life of all people influenced by it. The primary urge will be for marriage, the setting up of home and family. There will be no inner contentment until their "castle" has been established. Their concentrated energies will not only be directed towards establishing a home but also towards maintaining it, living in it and beautifying it. They rarely feel the need for holidays elsewhere as life in their homes is made into a perennial holiday. If they do go away, their subconscious minds draw them back home and they are indeed glad to be back when their holiday is over.

The high artistic appreciation of the 6 vibration is generally displayed in their homes, giving them an atmosphere of beauty, harmony and good taste. These are extroverted people who delight in congenial company and avoid solitude. The hospitality of all true Six people is renowned. The genuine matriarchs and patriarchs who exercise a powerful yet benign influence over a large family are found within this vibration. They seek no other ambition than to lovingly control and serve their families.

All Sixes who are well established in their domestic lives are motivated by a strong urge to extend their love and personal service into the community. Strong maternal and paternal instinct to guide, counsel and teach finds fulfilment in community activity. In personal relationships their almost total attachment to home and family must be recognised by their partners. It will not be possible to influence these people to adopt a shifting lifestyle.

Sixes have no inner drive for competition in the commercial world. Love of good food, physical comfort and enjoyment of artistic pleasures could be taken to extremes by the more negative types, at the expense of physical activity.

VIBRATION NUMBER 7
Inner Person

A continual pull away from social involvement and competition in the commercial world is experienced both consciously and subconsciously by subjects of this vibration. They feel a real need for silence and peace, which they find in solitude and communion with their inner selves. Strident noises and other discordant vibrations of the outer world have a deleterious effect on them. Much suffering is caused if they are constantly exposed to these disturbances. The situation is compounded when contrasting vibrations exist in the other Spheres of Influence. For instance, individuals with a 7 inner person will suffer much inner conflict if other Spheres of Influence are ruled by the extrovert social vibrations. Their greatest problem will be to reconcile these opposing facets of their personalities. Learning to be alone and not being lonely will be one of the first adjustments.

Quite often these individuals are depressed and deeply withdrawn and fail to realise the cause of their moods. Associates and loved ones will certainly be unable to do this and a good deal of unnecessary misunderstanding is caused as a result. These Sevens are not able to communicate their inner feelings to others. They find it most distasteful to expose their sentiments to others.

Those Sevens who are undisturbed by contrary vibrations within themselves are easily able to live alone. The absence of emotional attachments gives them the opportunity to devote themselves to spiritual unfoldment, which will often be their greatest wish.

VIBRATION NUMBER 8
Inner Person

The inner urges of the 8 vibration separate themselves into two distinct but not dissimilar forces. On the one hand, the desire to possess material wealth and power exerts pressure on the personality, and on the other hand the 8 vibration's natural tendencies to lead, organise and administer affairs and people, seek to take over. The combination of these two forces inevitably produces a forceful personality if outlets for expression are present in the other Spheres of Influence.

It is not an easy inner life to cope with, for opportunities for fulfilment may not always be presented and, furthermore, the destiny of an individual may point in a different direction. If one or more of the other spheres are not geared to handle these powerful forces, frustration need not necessarily be the result. Some of the strong attributes of the 8 vibration, such as enthusiasm for work, determination, dedication and organisation, can be used to achieve success in any other type of destiny, or they could be used for generally strengthening the personality type. The secret is to realise that these powers exist in the background of the personality. Although others will not recognise an 8 soul urge on outer appearances, they will soon do so when these people live up to all expectations and demands of life.

VIBRATION NUMBER 9
Inner Person

Stirred up by an emotional core, all Nines revel in high ideals and visions for the amelioration of animal and human suffering.

Their compulsion to contemplate on cruelty to animals, people's inhumanity to one another, and nature's harshness to both, creates within them a restlessness and a sense of urgency, followed by a need for action. These altruistic promptings often clash with their ambition and wishes for personal enrichment through material possessions. Successful Nine personalities overcome the drawbacks of self-centredness, selfishness and emotionalism and are able to concentrate on humanitarian service. Their strongest urge is to become the universal brother or universal sister.

The refined vibrations animating these people give them proficiency and love for music, art, drama and literature, which enables them to express their fine sensitivity, high sense of beauty and high-minded thoughts. Favoured by the internationalism of the 9 vibration they instinctively regard the world as their stage and seek knowledge of and participation in the cultural pursuits of all lands. There is a strong drive to undertake frequent journeys to the cultural centres of the world and to acquire for themselves the reputation as ambassadors of learning.

The generosity of the 9 vibration constantly erupts and is displayed not in the dispensation of material largesse but in personal service as teachers, healers, humanitarians and philanthrophists. The desire to give, even at the expense of their own impoverishment, leads these people into many difficult situations.

Their inner desires are not confined to cultural and humanitarian pursuits but also include to a large extent spiritual unfoldment. Their religious beliefs are not often of the traditional type. Global orientation, intuition and extrasensory perception guide them into the widest possible fields of knowledge in metaphysics and mysticism. The need to impart this knowledge soon takes over.

VIBRATION NUMBER 11
Inner Person

The vibrations that agitate the inner life of people whose vowels add up to 11 are an escalation of those represented by the number 9. This escalation applies particularly in regard to internationalism and the dissemination of spiritual knowledge. The sensitivity and emotion of the Nines have been largely overcome at this stage and the Elevens are capable of emotional detachment.

Their inner life is spent in enjoyment of their visions and dreams for upliftment of the spiritual and moral life of humanity as a whole, with little or no concern for individuals. Their passion to reveal what they, rightly or wrongly, consider are the true remedies for the salvation of humanity is irresistible. This is followed by a call to evangelise. With the strength of two 1's and the support of the underlying 2, inner guidance is at its strongest with these individuals. They can safely rely upon their intuition and psychic ability. Their devotion, strength and single-mindedness make them entirely fearless in probing the spiritual and physical realms of life, and also in resisting any onslaughts upon their ideals and visions.

While some Elevens will confine themselves to theorising and spreading the "Word" as they see it, without practical application, others may seek to direct their considerable inner powers towards inventions that may remain as lasting aids to human welfare. The degree of success achieved will no doubt depend upon the other Spheres of Influence.

In negative Eleven personalities their message is delivered in an egoistic and pedantic manner with little concern for the sensitivities and opinions of others. In intimate relationships all Elevens, whether positive or negative, reveal themselves as serious individuals engaged in a wide spectrum of idealism with little time and concern for personal responsibilities.

VIBRATION NUMBER 22
Inner Person

People activated from within by this Master vibration of the "master builder" seek means for practical application of their spiritual, mental and physical energies. They realise that thought and speech must be followed by constructive deeds. Thought processes of these people have an extraordinary power to create or destroy and they are so intense that they influence the lives of those around them.

Very few individuals realise the demands of this powerful and comprehensive vibration. Those who do not realise them have the 4 vibration as their inner self.

The most ardent wish of all positive people with the 22 inner urge is to see a society of nations and to play a considerable part in contributing some lasting benefit to this vast organisation. Their thoughts are projected into international organisations of various sorts, humanitarian societies, the construction of buildings on a large scale, roads, railways, waterways, and the development of aerial and space travel. Negative people unfortunately are insensitive to the welfare of others and direct their powerful creative thoughts towards selfish accumulation of power and wealth.

FIRST VOWEL OF THE GIVEN NAME

The given name, or name most often used, provides an interesting development through the power of its first vowel and this, more often than not, provides the first insight into the personality of an individual. The first vowel determines an individual's immediate impulses, responses and reactions to all outer stimuli and in most people gives an instant revelation of their basic personality type.

Once the governing vibration of the vowel is known, not only will the reactions of others to orders, questions, proposals and other occurrences be understood, but also how best to approach them, thereby obtaining the most favourable response.

The characteristics of the first vowel are emphasised when it is the first letter in the name and has a sound vibration of a long duration, as in Andrew or Andrea. As the second letter but still with a long duration, as in Dale or Dora, the power of the vowel will be influenced to a degree by the vibration of the first letter, though retaining a good deal of its individual strength. The influence of the vowel is lessened when the sound is crisp, as in Roger or Doris, and the resulting reactions are milder. The union of two vowel sounds, as in Neal or Pauline, will complicate matters a little by the introduction of the influence of two vibrations expressed as one.

While the influence of the first vowel is helpful, it is only a cursory view of personality. It should not be used independently to judge people and needs to be combined with the information of as many of the Six Spheres of Influence as possible for a defined picture.

FIRST VOWEL A
Number 1

Reactions are mental as well as emotional, but emotions are not displayed due to the strong self-restraint of the 1 vibration which the letter *a* represents. Subject to the position of the vowel and the duration of its sound, these people will show:

1. Receptivity to new ideas and activities on account of the 1 vibration's desire to create, pioneer and explore.
2. A negative reaction to orders, advice and opinions of others since they would rather give orders, learn by experience and voice their own opinions.
3. A hostile reaction to criticism and a challenge by others of their ideas, opinions and instructions.
4. Strong resentment of any intrusion upon their privacy.
5. Intolerance of stagnant or non-progressive views.
6. Accessibility only by straightforward means and impatience and distrust of people who use a devious approach.

FIRST VOWEL E
Number 5

Reaction to all outer stimuli is the swiftest with this vowel owing to the 5 vibration's ever present alertness, awareness and inner agitation.

1. As all five senses work together with this vibration these people miss nothing and caution should be exercised by others in speech and action when these Fives are around.
2. Reactions are impulsive. Promises and concurrences given by them on the spur of the moment should not be taken seriously because they could easily change their minds. They also have a strong tendency to overact and to overdramatise events.
3. They are easily accessible and influenced by an emotional approach and are very receptive to novelty, variety and intrigue.
4. Impatience is displayed to those whose thought processes and movements are slow and to those who constantly repeat themselves.
5. Strong reactions are shown towards anyone who attempts to place any restrictions upon their freedom.
6. They are freely approachable by members of the opposite sex since no inhibitions or fears are held by these people.

FIRST VOWEL I
Number 9

A wide perspective is used in the realm of thought by these people. Pettiness and prejudices are their pet aversions.

1. Intuition, sensitivity, emotion and refinement influence all their reactions.
2. All their judgements are made by universal standards.

3. They are accessible and accommodating and easily moved by appeals for sympathy. Generosity is spontaneous.
4. Instant displeasure is shown towards aggressiveness and crudeness.
5. The negative personalities produce very different reactions, such as boredom, moodiness, cynicism and selfishness. They could be obnoxious and hurtful both intentionally and un-intentionally.

FIRST VOWEL *O*
Number 6

Traditionalists and conservatives are found here. Home, family and loved ones are their first priority. Approached along these lines, they will be congenial, hospitable and helpful.

1. Being strongly influenced by the vibration of guardianship and protection, they will react instantly to any danger that may face their charges.
2. In all other instances, their responses are not immediate; they need to deliberate before giving their consent or opinion on any matter.
3. The mental approach to these people is best as logic governs their thoughts, and irritation will soon be displayed with emotional and erratic speech and unstable behaviour. They will promptly raise an argument if a statement or opinion by someone does not conform with facts. As a result, they often create unpleasantness although their intention is merely to help others get their facts right.
4. They find it difficult to control their constant urge to teach, advise and counsel.
5. People motivating negatively are self-opinionated and dogmatic and react fiercely to any challenge to their opinions and instructions. Their general responses are moody and melancholy.

FIRST VOWEL *U*
Number 3

A ready sense of humour forms the basis for most of their responses. They are so quick at repartee that there is a need to watch what is said to them, especially by shy or sensitive people. They are always on the alert for humorous situations and will swiftly respond to an ordinary remark with a witty retort.

1. Their most powerful weapon is the gift of speech, which is used generally in friendship, though they could be cutting and satirical if they choose to be.

2. Their reactions are enthusiastic, optimistic and animated. Beauty and colour instantly catch their eye.

3. There is no need to repeat or explain anything in detail to these people. They pick up new facts and information instantly, much to the amazement of slower thinking people around them.

4. They respond eagerly to personal love, adulation and flattery. This will the best approach for receiving their friendship and loyalty. The negative ones who may not receive these attentions will create situations to do so. This urgent need leads them easily into many emotional escapades and makes them prey to all types of other influences.

5. An instant response is given to pets and children.

FIRST VOWEL Y
Number 7

This is rarely the first vowel, but when it is, the deeper characteristics of the 7 vibration will be displayed. The names Yvonne and Yves are examples.

1. Their aversion to frivolous and superficial people will not be concealed, while their attraction to and admiration for deep-thinking and learned people will be openly displayed.

2. Attempts to obtain any information from them, especially of a personal nature, usually ends in disappointment and embarrassment, for they will not reveal anything about themselves. They are enigmatic and often misunderstood.

3. A display of emotion or conduct that does not conform to reason will either raise their ire or see them withdraw within themselves.

4. Their attention and ready response is always gained if some serious or philosophical matter is broached and discussed objectively.

THE SIXTH SPHERE OF INFLUENCE
CONSONANTS OF THE WHOLE NAME

The existence of an inner realm within our personality must, by the law of opposites, indicate the existence of an outer realm. The single digit resulting from the sum of the consonants of the whole name is the clue that distinguishes the outer from the inner. The outer realm is also referred to as the outer person. The vibrations of the physical body play a significant part in this Sphere of Influence.

This aspect of the integral personality is projected outwards both consciously and unconsciously. It is the area of first impressions and may be regarded as a facade, mask or image we present to others, from which their initial judgements are made. Herein lies the importance of the Sixth Sphere of Influence. Though not always representative of our true selves, we should be aware of the characteristics presented by this sphere and use them consciously and honestly as a medium by which we may conduct ourselves in the most advantageous manner. The collective features of this sphere can very well be the secret of our success in the many varied situations in which we may find ourselves. It could also be used to deceive others as well as ourselves, but any success achieved by this means will be short-lived, for the true personality will emerge sooner or later.

The Sixth Sphere is the one area of our personality complex that needs constant attention and updating because it is from here that our mannerisms, speech, dress, posture and other outward habits and idiosyncrasies are displayed. Once again, recognition, reconciliation and balance of this Sixth Sphere with the other spheres should be a significant consideration. We need to recognise that this Outer Sphere should work in harmony with our composite personality as determined by the other five Spheres of Influence. As such, the Sixth Sphere should reflect this whole identity rather than simply aligning itself with frequently changing fashions and conventions which may not always suit our individual personalities.

The inner and outer spheres of influence should always be considered in conjunction with each other. The outer person could be quite deceiving as it often serves consciously and unconsciously to obscure the inner person, which may be insecure and fearful, or, on the contrary, strong and resilient. Many an attractive outer person may hide a weak and wayward character, while a person of ability and sterling character may lie behind an unattractive and seemingly dull outer person.

An individual possessing an attractive outer person, and knowing it, may by all means take advantage of its gifts, but if these gifts are not backed up by supportive vibrations in the other Spheres of Influence, he or she will eventually overplay their part or fail to live up to expectations. On the other hand, people realising that their outer person may be unattractive and dull may fail to sell themselves though they may be individuals of many talents. We also encounter people whose outer and inner spheres of influence are of the same numbers. These are straightforward personalities who are in fact exactly what they appear to be.

The following words from Robert Burns' "Lines to a Louse" come to mind when discussing this Outer Sphere:

O wad some power the giftie gie us
To see oursels as others see us!
It wad frae mony a blunder free us
And foolish notion.

In order to ascertain the outer person of Percival Smith, we shall convert the consonants of his whole name as follows:

P	E	R	C	I	V	A	L		E	D	W	A	R	D		S	M	I	T	H
7		9	3		4		3			4	5			9	4		1	4		2	8

$$26 \qquad\qquad 22 \qquad\qquad 15$$

$$8 \quad + \quad 4 \quad + \quad 6 = 18 = 9$$

With the number 9 controlling his outer person, Percival projects the image of a high-minded individual with a comprehensive outlook. Unless supported by other areas of influence, he will find it difficult to maintain this image at all times, and support is not strong. His inner person, which is ruled by the younger 3 vibration, may not always be able to keep up with the projected appearances of the maturer 9, nor will the 2 vibration forming his personality type help. Although both the 3 and 2 vibrations are versatile and adaptable they belong to the ego-centred group and it will not be easy for these spheres of influence to match the image of the true Nine personality.

VIBRATION NUMBER 1
Outer Person

Typical 1 vibration qualities of individuality, authority, will-power, resourcefulness, courage and new ideas will be projected by those whose outer person is governed by this vibration. Their speech and general manner will be direct and matter-of-fact, and their individuality will also be reflected in their attire, which will always be neat, stylish, personal and exclusive.

They will quickly attract the regard and acceptance by others of the characteristics they present. However, a corresponding backup by similar vibrations in the other spheres of influence will be needed in order to maintain the personality type projected. If not, there will be a let down in a crisis, leading to failure and disappointment.

VIBRATION NUMBER 2
Outer Person

The effects produced on others will be a fine mixture of refinement, gentleness, tact, patience and harmony. People will feel comfortable in the presence of these non-aggressive personalities and will enjoy the reassuring presence of associates and helpers rather than critics and competitors.

The impression of kindliness and understanding these personalities exude make them popular in social life. Strongly active characters are instantly attracted to these types. They are soft-spoken, graceful and rhythmical in their movements and look their best in garments made of soft, flowing materials.

VIBRATION NUMBER 3
Outer Person

These individuals are seen as friendly, good humoured, vivacious and entertaining; they are depended upon to lead the conversation in any gathering. Not surprisingly, they find themselves the centre of attention, lifting the atmosphere to a level that gives pleasure to all those present. They project high intelligence, alertness, youthfulness and comradeship. This is a frontal appearance that has many demands placed on it, especially in the social scene.

Always fashionably dressed, many Threes are known for their outrageous styles, accessories and colours. Their artistic flair and youthful deportment make them look well in almost any style and colour.

VIBRATION NUMBER 4
Outer Person

A composite image of respectability, conservatism and patriotism is projected by people with this outer aspect. In addition, the comfortable and secure atmosphere around them, on account of their dependability, practicality and commonsense, influences many people to attach themselves to these Four personalities.

Their honest and kindly manner may be somewhat coloured by sternness, self-discipline and forthright speech. Healthy physical energy dedicated to work and service to others will be their most prominent feature. Great trust and reliance will always be placed on them by others. Clothing chosen by them will be for durability and quality rather than for colour, flamboyance and fashion.

VIBRATION NUMBER 5
Outer Person

The reputation of these people as the greatest talkers will be well known. Enthusiasm, emotion, wit and repartee characterise their speech, making them influential and interesting conversationalists. They are relied upon by others to keep conversation alive in any gathering. The more negative ones could carry this gift of speech too far and plunge headlong into discussing matters they know very little about.

They project strong personal magnetism and sensuality, and other typical traits of the 5 vibration such as impulsiveness, daring and nervous energy. A fast turnover in relationships can be expected. While they are easily bored and seek change, many people may find it wearisome to put up with their highly tensed vibrations for very long. As leaders of fashion they are well dressed and often display the daring of the 5 vibration in their choice of clothes and colour.

VIBRATION NUMBER 6
Outer Person

The paternal or maternal look distinguishes the Six outer person from others. Sympathy and understanding are expressed in their speech and manner. People of all ages do not hesitate to seek their company for they are seen as basically good people who are approachable and helpful. And since all Sixes love to be of service to others they would never disappoint or rebuff anyone. Their patience, tact and diplomacy give them the ability to handle all types of people.

In dress, they are more concerned with comfort than following the latest fashions. Garments of good quality and simple styles will be their choice, rather than anything intricate and fussy.

VIBRATION NUMBER 7
Outer Person

People with Seven outer personalities stand out in a crowd by their aloofness and poise. An air of mystery and distance surrounds them. As their oral communication is strictly controlled, very little is known about their thoughts. They give an impression of unapproachability and exclusiveness and as a result are often misunderstood by those who do not know them well. Often unfair interpretations are placed on their manner and speech, especially their indifference to casual conversation.

All Sevens unconsciously project an image, often quite justifiably, of being intelligent and knowledgeable people. They will not be seen in flashy clothes and gaudy colours. Sober colours and quality materials will be their choice.

VIBRATION NUMBER 8
Outer Person

Eight outer persons will display an image of prosperity, success, authority and power, plus many of the popular characteristics of the 8 vibration. As a result, these personalities frequently find themselves in positions of authority and responsibility. However, they need to be backed up by supportive inner vibrations and other strong personality traits. If not, the strong facade they project will be no more than a false front leading to an inevitable let down. If there is good backing, openings for advancement and success will always be offered to them.

They are conservative in their choice of clothing and regardless of their circumstances dress in a manner which conveys an aura of prosperity.

VIBRATION NUMBER 9
Outer Person

Personal magnetism without the slightest degree of aggression or egotism is projected by these individuals. They are seen as kindly and worldly-wise people who are understanding and approachable and are welcome in any gathering for their wide knowledge and conversational skills.

Their innate wisdom and ability to fraternise easily attracts all types of people who, no matter what their status, feel comfortable and eager in the presence of Nines, rather than inferior and uninformed.

Nines are also seen as emotional and romantic people and could have many admirers among the opposite sex. Their internationalism is also seen in their dress. They do not hesitate to wear anything that is comfortable, dramatic, colourful and artistically put together.

VIBRATION NUMBER 11
Outer Person

Depending on the presence or absence of stability in the other Spheres of Influence, these Elevens will appear either as inspirational, mystical and high-minded, or as dreamers, fanatics, soapbox preachers and phonies. Whether positive or negative in outlook, all Elevens will make use of every opportunity to give vocal expression to their insights and opinions, which are always ahead of the times and even revolutionary. They do not hesitate to express strong opinions on equality of the sexes and equality of opportunity. Their tendency towards exaggeration and elaboration is well known to their listeners.

As originators rather than followers, particularly in the fine arts, their individuality is seen in their clothing. Most Elevens would prefer to make or design their own clothes so that their artistic flair may be given expression.

VIBRATION NUMBER 22
Outer Person

Positive personalities with a 22 vibration controlling their outer image will be seen as commanding personalities with an aura of power and control over all situations. Physical and mental energy, practicality, efficiency and expertise in any field are characteristics displayed by them. They are familiar figures in the international scene, dressed in the highest quality clothing in conservative styles and always appearing successful and wealthy.

This is a difficult facade for the average personality to maintain. The vibrations of the Four outer person are seen in those who are unable to keep up with the high image of this Master vibration.

This chapter completes the information on the Six Spheres of Influence. By analysing the details presented by each sphere, a complex, composite image can be created of the person being studied. It is always important to develop an understanding of the interrelations of the numbers and the way particular numbers in combination have particular ways of influencing each other.

We have outlined many factors which affect the relationships of the numbers. These include the presence or absence of the 1 vibration, the repetition of numbers, conflict between particular Spheres of Influence, conflict between planes of expression, the absence of numbers in particular areas of the birth grid and similarities between numbers.

The following chapters are designed to help develop greater insight into the relationships of the numbers, which in turn will strengthen our ability to make more accurate numerological assessments of the people we meet and wish to analyse.

THE SIGNIFICANCE OF THE
LETTERS OF THE WHOLE NAME

The letters of the whole name fulfil another important function by contributing complementary sets of vibrations to be considered in relation to those of the birth date. Although their influence is not as powerful as the First, Second and Third Spheres of Influence, they contribute significantly towards the personality as a whole. The letters, with their corresponding number values, may be found in a manner that could provide areas of power that are not found in the birth date; could strengthen vibrations existing in the birth date; and could overload an individual with a particular vibration.

The numerological grid is again used to set up a picture using the letter/numbers of the whole name. We record the number of times each letter/number appears and then consider the pattern that has unfolded, as in the following example:

Date of birth: 20 . 12 . 1938 = 26 = 8

Birth date grid

3		9
2<u>2</u>		8<u>8</u>
1 1 0		

P E R C I V A L   E D W A R D   S M I T H
7 5 9 3 9 4 1 3   5 4 5 1 9 4   1 4 9 2 8

Number of times vibrations appear in the whole name

1 — 3	4 — 4	7 — 1
2 — 1	5 — 3	8 — 1
3 — 2	6 — –	9 — 4

The Fixed grid

3	6	9	Mental
2	5	8	Emotional
1	4	7	Physical

Whole name grid for Percival Edward Smith

2	–	4
1	3	1
3	4	1

We may now consider the grid of the whole name with the grid of the birth date and see what advantages and disadvantages are contained within the letters of the whole name. We may commence by considering the horizontal and vertical areas and then the individual squares.

The physical plane, which is not strong in the birth date, has received welcome support from eight letters or vibrations. The emotional plane, strong in the birth date, has not been overloaded. The power of the mental plane has been increased considerably, but not to the point of overloading.

The first vertical area (1, 2, 3) shows that six well-placed numbers have provided potential for individuality, willpower, creative imagination and leadership — qualities not found in the birth date.

The seven letters in the second area (4, 5, 6), though not spread over all three squares, have helped considerably since this sphere is blank in the birth date. The 4s have given balance on the practical side, especially valuable in the domestic scene where it can fill in for the 6 vibration which is lacking in both the birth date and the whole name. There are three vital 5s. At least two more would have been better, for this is the number of experience and without it an individual shows little or no interest in participating in even the ordinary experiences of life.

The six letters of the third vertical area (7, 8, 9) provide good balance. The single 7 vibration is more than adequate to fulfil a balancing role in its area of the grid since not many 7s appear in names. The single 8 is also good as this area of his personality is strengthened through the vibrations of his birth date. The four 9s help considerably in widening the thought processes of this individual who is essentially egocentric.

We may now consider how the personality has been affected by the numbers, or their absence, in the individual squares, though some repetition is inevitable.

1. The 1 vibration in three letters has added strength to the personality.

2. The 2 vibration, strong in the birth date, is not overloaded.

3. The presence of the 3 vibration in two letters is advantageous and gives roundness to the personality. The 3 in the birth date is not strong.

4. The 4 vibration, not present in the birth date, is found here to a degree that will certainly help the personality on the practical plane.

5. The 5 vibration is not present in the birth date and is not strong enough in the whole name to be of substantial help. Five or more would have been helpful. The lack of strength in this area will produce a restricting effect on the personality as a whole.

6. The 6 vibration is not present in the birth date and is not found in the letters of the whole name either. Though the specific 6 qualities will be lacking, there will be compensation from the strong 2 vibrations in the birth date and 4 vibrations in the whole name as these share many characteristics with the 6.

7. The single 7 is advantageous as it gives roundness to the personality.

8. The single 8 is also advantageous as it, too, gives roundness to the personality without causing stress through overloading.
9. The 9 vibration is strong in the letters and will have a definite influence on the personality.

In the following pages each number from 1 to 9 is taken in turn and their influence in the whole name grid in relation to the birth grid is described. The effect the name has in balancing and harmonising the birth date or compounding its problems is detailed.

These interpretations emphasise the importance of making a careful choice when selecting a name for a baby, or the problems that may be alleviated if adults choose to change their name to help balance their birth date.

It should be remembered that the negative traits become more significant if the number under discussion does not appear anywhere in the whole name, the birth date, or in any of the six Spheres of Influence. However, some numbers possess similar characteristics and the loss or absence of the qualities of a particular vibration need not be total. For instance, the absence of the 3 vibration indicates difficulties with oral expression, but this will be compensated for if the 5 vibration is found in strength. Also, it should be noted that while the absence of a number in the birth chart can be rectified by an abundance of this number in the whole name grid, the abundance of a number in both the birth grid and the whole name grid will result in negative traits of that particular number taking hold of the personality.

VIBRATION NUMBER 1
A, J, S

People whose birth dates do not have the 1 vibration present in any degree of strength will find it most advantageous if their names have a total of three or four letters which convert to this number. In the following example, neither the birth date nor the surname provide the desirable 1 vibration, except the weak century 1, but a wise choice of the given name and middle name has equipped the personality with a total of four letters of the 1 vibration:

Birth date: 24 . 3 . 1944 = 27 = 9

S U S A N   J O Y C E   H U N T E R
1   1 1   1

This individual will not miss out on the driving force of the primeval vibration and its many other fundamental characteristics, such as independent thought, ambition, leadership and, above all, self-confidence.

Generally, the absence of this number in both the birth date and letters of the whole name will cause problems, but before a final opinion is formed a further search should be made in the chart for its presence or absence in the other Spheres of Influence. For instance, this vibration as the outer person in the Sixth Sphere of Influence will not carry the individual very far, but as the inner person in the Fifth Sphere, there is an assurance that strong personality traits are present deep within and these may eventually break through.

The total absence of the 1 vibration is an indication of an inferiority complex and a dormant ego. Because they do not trust themselves, these people will lack initiative, ambition and independence and automatically become followers who will gladly let others make their decisions for them. The younger ones will be dominated and influenced at home and school — a situation that will not boost their self-esteem. With maturity they may eventually acquire some measure of self-confidence and self-sufficiency.

VIBRATION NUMBER 2
B, K, T

The best attributes of the 2 vibration will be present in a whole name containing three of these letters. The ability to see an opposite point of view and to cooperate, will be the principal advantages. Other qualities, such as tact, diplomacy, friendliness and sensitivity, will also be contributed and will be most beneficial in the case of birth dates with many active numbers showing aggression.

If the 2 vibration is strong in the First Sphere of Influence and is also found in abundance in the whole name, that is, four or more letters, sensitivity and emotionalism will tend to be emphasised. It could lead to effeminacy in men and extreme shyness and abnormal fears in women. However, both sexes will have a strong feeling for beauty and delicacy in all things and will express many talents in the fine arts.

The absence of understanding, uncooperativeness, lack of consideration and tactlessness are failings in people who do not have this vibration in their birth dates or names. Lessons they need to learn are attention to detail, and punctuality. The situation is alleviated to some extent in a positive Six personality (First Sphere of Influence).

VIBRATION NUMBER 3
C, L, U

Self-expression through the gift of speech and a sense of humour will be noteworthy characteristics of people with these letters in proportion. Talent will also be displayed in the creative arts. Imagination, inspiration, creativity, gaiety and optimism will be basic qualities.

People with an abundance of these letters — four or more — may take the good qualities of the 3 vibration to extremes and lose a sense of balance and responsibility. Their energies may be dissipated and emotional disturbances revealed in extreme talkativeness. Self-centredness and waywardness may be reflected in all their thoughts and actions.

The lack of the 3 vibration in the names, with no support in the birth date, results in inhibition of many of this vibration's outstanding attributes. A strong 5 vibration will help overcome difficulties experienced in oral expression and social intercourse. If the 1 vibration is not strong in the overall structure these people will choose to undersell themselves rather than make any attempt at self-promotion.

VIBRATION NUMBER 4
D, M, V

People with mentally and emotionally oriented vibrations in their birth dates benefit considerably from the letters D, M and V in their names. Three to four letters of the 4 vibration give them balance, a sense of values, willingness to perform physical tasks, ability to handle money wisely and practicality.

An abundance of these letters, especially if the number 4 is strong in the birth date, will produce stubbornness, narrow-mindedness and lack of imagination.

If the names do not provide this vibration and there is no support in the birth date, the direct result will be a dislike and fear of physical work or any activity that requires orderly manual effort. These individuals will develop a slipshod attitude and avoid system, timetables and routine. They will resort to short cuts in order to overcome or minimise attention to basic duties. The affairs of these people are usually in a state of confusion and as a result may resort to escapism. The presence of the 1 vibration or the 7 will help overcome some of these problems.

VIBRATION NUMBER 5
E, N, W

As the only vibration that communicates with every facet of the personality, a generous proportion of letters is needed before it is strong enough to reach out and influence the personality as a whole. Four to six letters will see the effects of its general features, the best being the capacity to handle an active life involving change, travel and experience.

People whose names do not contain these letters, or who have one or two only, have real problems with motivation and involvement in activity of any form. Curiosity, which is natural to human nature, is not found in these people. They also suffer from lack of tolerance and are stolid and unadaptable. They become introverted and constantly seek seclusion, content to live totally dull and negative lives. Their fear of the opposite sex is considerable. In short, they find it extremely difficult to adapt to ordinary living. Life usually forces them out of their lethargy and fears to some extent, though they will continue to suffer much internal turmoil.

Misuse of personal freedom resulting in possible hurt to others will be a problem with those with an overabundance of 5's in their birth date as well as their names. The desire for a variety of sensual experiences is very strong in these people.

VIBRATION NUMBER 6
F, O, X

A total of three letters will see the loving nature of the 6 vibration displayed at its best and will ensure its natural capacity for domestic harmony, responsible parenthood, teaching and community service.

An excess of these letters, unfortunately, brings a rigid unyielding attitude. Self-righteousness becomes a real problem, along with over-concern for domestic issues.

People whose names are without these letters will show irresponsibility in the domestic scene. The fear of being tied down and abnormal concern for self will provide genuine problems for people associated with them. There will be little or no understanding, tolerance or sympathy in their roles as partners, parents or guardians. Many personal adjustments will have to be made by them in order to succeed as marriage partners and community-conscious citizens. They will need to learn to give, especially of themselves, before they can expect to receive. This situation will be relieved somewhat if the personalities are controlled by positive 2 or 4 vibrations.

VIBRATION NUMBER 7
G, P, Y

These letters do not occur frequently. One or two may be regarded as proportionate. The presence of these letters stirs the intuitive faculty, which in turn influences the thoughts and actions of the individual. There is an instinctive acceptance of Divinity and a spiritual basis for all existence. The 7 vibration's love of analysis, research and clear-cut facts will also be present.

An excess of these letters is rare. If found, they would force the individual to withdraw from society and resort to some form of escapism.

Unless support is found in the birth date, the absence of faith, indifference to spiritual values leading to a fear of the non-material, are familiar characteristics of those people who have missed out on these letters.

A mental laziness is present in so far as all abstract matters are concerned. These people are often jolted out of their lethargy by a sudden personal calamity, which may force them to turn inward for questioning and guidance. This inward search may eventually develop faith in more enduring values and help them overcome their fear, scepticism and doubt. The 9 vibration found in strength will help overcome some of these problems.

VIBRATION NUMBER 8
H, Q, Z

These are also letters that do not occur frequently. However, two to three are needed for an individual to have the 8 vibration's basic attributes. A good sense of values in the material world, backed up by good judgement, will be the main contributions.

The ambitions of people with an abundance of these letters will exceed their capabilities and opportunities. Constant anxiety will be experienced in their attempts to keep abreast of the demands of their ambition.

As judgement is one of the strongest attributes of the 8 vibration, the absence of this vibration shows poor judgement in most matters, particularly in finance. People in this situation have no control or competence in the disposition of their income and other assets. Financial problems will always be present until they are forced by circumstances to learn proper management of their affairs and to live within their means. The 4 or the 7 vibration in control of the personality will overcome poor judgement in these matters.

VIBRATION NUMBER 9
I, R

A total of two or three of these letters is adequate to provide the 9 vibration's most important attributes of humanitarianism and internationalism.

An abundance of either or both of these letters, which is not common, will cause a fear and over-concern for the problems of the world. Such people have a dismal outlook which spreads bad vibrations around, affecting their own health and the well-being of those associated with them.

Self-centredness will be the problem with people who have missed out on these letters. They will have little or no understanding of the human aspects of life and will prefer to remain detached from the troubles of others. Suffering will not move them. This situation is overcome to some extent by the presence of a good proportion of the 6 vibration in the names.

Personal relationships will also be difficult owing to hardened emotional attitudes. Unless these individuals begin to soften from within and accept involvement with people, sharing their joys and sorrows, a lonely life will be their lot.

THE COMPATIBILITY OF NUMBERS

The final chapter contains brief comments on the compatibility of numbers in relation to business and personal association. It is meant to be an instant guide only and if an elaboration of these comments is required, reference should be made to the chapters on the First, Second and Fifth Spheres of Influence.

When a comparison is made between two people to ascertain the degree of compatibility, particular care should be taken to confine the examination only to corresponding spheres. The First Sphere of one should be compared with the First Sphere of the other, or the Fifth Sphere of one with the Fifth Sphere of the other. The mixing of spheres will only cause confusion.

A much deeper study into the number pattern will be required to discover whether some measure of compatibility exists or can be developed if similiar numbers are found in different spheres. For instance, compatibility cannot be taken for granted if a personality named John is a Six type (First Sphere) and a personality named Helen is a Six — inner person (Fifth Sphere). John's 6 characteristics will actively control his personality while in Helen they will be in a passive state or in a condition of yearning only, and may remain so if her personality type is a Five.

The personality type (First Sphere) with the aid of the outer person (Sixth Sphere) is for the most part responsible for initial attraction, which more often than not may develop into a long-term association. However, to be certain of this development, compatibility of the vibrations of the inner person (Fifth Sphere) should be checked. These two spheres are at the same time tied up with the Sphere of Destiny (Second Sphere). All three spheres are therefore equally important and need to be considered together to ascertain the degree of compatibility and the amount and type of adjustments that invariably have to be made.

ONE AND ONE

An unlikely and undesirable combination in a personal relationship. In the event of this occurring the relationship will not go beyond its incipient stage. Two strong-willed and independent characters will not be prepared to surrender any part of their individuality to each other. A personality clash is certain. However, a business partnership could be made very successful if each party has independent functions and they work together only when competing with others.

ONE AND TWO

There is a magnetic attraction between people influenced by these active and receptive vibrations. One will complement the other by providing what the other does not possess and needs. A strong bond will develop between these two once each other's role is understood. An excellent combination in both personal and business partnerships.

ONE AND THREE

In personal relationships, problems are inevitable between these ego-centred individuals. Competition between the two will be constant. Both parties will give orders. The Ones will not tolerate the easy lifestyle of the Threes and the Threes, in turn, will not stand by and accept the dominance of the Ones. However, this combination could be a powerful force in business provided they have departments of their own, with the Threes taking the reins in the foreground and the Ones holding power in the background.

ONE AND FOUR

A very workable relationship in personal life as well as in business. The Ones will respect the dependability, practicality and honesty of the Fours, while the Fours will happily follow the creativity and decisiveness of the Ones. A strong bond will be forged between them once the Ones have learned to tolerate the deliberation of the Fours and the Fours have become accustomed to the rapidity of the thought processes of the Ones.

ONE AND FIVE

A powerful and successful combination can be formed here, both in business and personal life. The extrovert and alert Five complements the inventive One. The One will produce while the Five organises, advertises and sells. Fear of any sort will not influence their activities. Their lives could develop into a great adventure. The Five should respect the One's individuality and take care not to organise this partner's life. The One should not attempt to restrict the freedom of movement which is inherent in the Five.

ONE AND SIX

A worthwhile relationship can be worked out with this combination. Rough edges found in the personalities of many Ones can be removed by the genial and culture loving Sixes. The Six will appreciate the support the One is certain to give in the domestic scene. Sixes should be careful not to confine the Ones to an excess of domesticity. Many arguments will arise in this relationship due to the logic of the Sixes and the single-mindedness of the Ones. A successful business partnership could be achieved. Both parties will use their heads instead of their hearts in all their dealings.

ONE AND SEVEN

There is a natural attraction here and one of the strongest possible associations can be formed once each party understands each other's individuality and need for privacy. One party should not be too demanding of the other. The One in particular should refrain from the natural urge to give orders. Success of their association will be built upon mutual respect of each other's mental ability and efficiency.

ONE AND EIGHT

This could be a disastrous personal combination unless fundamental adjustments are made. Both parties will seek to establish power and authority over the other. On the other hand this could be formed into the most powerful of all business associations with each having an area of responsibility for the exercise of their expertise.

ONE AND NINE

After some mutual adjustments, a wide ranging and fruitful association can be achieved by these two personalities whose numbers are placed at the opposite ends of the number spectrum. The ideas of the ego-centred Ones will clash with the universal Nines. On the other hand, the wisdom and understanding of the Nines can temper and absorb the Ones' head-on drive for personal gain.

ONE AND ELEVEN

An improbable combination. The physically and materially oriented Ones will not put up with the idealism and impracticality of the Elevens. The Elevens' attempts to reform the Ones' attitudes will be treated with scorn. The Elevens will find it difficult to cope with the self-centredness and acquisitive traits of the Ones.

ONE AND TWENTY-TWO

This is a powerful combination. The Ones will find that they have met more than their match. They will accept the genius of the positive Twenty-twos and the Twenty-twos in turn will appreciate and use the initiative and energy of the Ones. This will turn out to be a combination of the Inventor and Builder.

TWO AND ONE

Same as One and Two.

TWO AND TWO

These are "birds of a feather who will flock together". Mutual understanding, giving and receiving, peace and harmony and much happiness will combine to form a great personal relationship. On the negative side, both parties will lack decisiveness and self-assertiveness. For these reasons, a business association should be avoided, unless a third party who is a One, Three or Five is included.

TWO AND THREE

A rewarding association can be formed once both parties understand their mutual need for personal attention — the Three to be deferred to and the Two to be cared for. The Two's shyness, sensitivity and reticence must be understood and accepted by the Three. The active, extrovert Threes can work successfully with the behind-the-scenes activity of the Twos; the Three being the go-getter and the Two the quiet achiever. The Three's flirtatious nature will cause some concern to the Two in a permanent relationship. However, the Two is not entirely immovable in emotional matters if strong persuasion is used by a third party.

TWO AND FOUR

A comfortable and stable association is assured, for these two have many characteristics in common. In addition, the imagination and fluidity of the Two will help open out the stay-put attitudes of the Four. The Four in turn will bring stability into the emotional life of the Two. Competition will not exist between them. One will always try to help the other. Success can be achieved both in personal and business relationships.

TWO AND FIVE

Problems are inevitable between these two emotionally charged personalities — one sensitive and easily hurt, the other volatile and callous of the other's feelings. The speed of the Five will bewilder the placid Two. The constant personal attention the Two needs will not be given by the Five. The Five in turn will be irritated by the Two's personal demands and attempts to restrict freedom of movement. If any measure of success is attained in this association it will be the result of adjustments by the Two.

TWO AND SIX

Love of peace and harmony will act as a magnet to bring these two together. There will be no competition here, nor will one try to overrule the other. Love of home will be their strongest bond, plus mutual interests in healing and other cultural pursuits. The logic of the Six will steady the sentimentality of the Two, while the Two will give co-operation and understanding to the Six. Personal happiness is assured. Success in business is also certain if they confine themselves to the many areas where they share expertise.

TWO AND SEVEN

Another promising combination. A few minor adjustments will be needed. The Two will have to accustom himself or herself to the Seven's need for periods of solitude and for the Seven's distaste for constant talk. The Seven should be tolerant of the Two's displays of emotion. The psychic talents of the Two will be appreciated by the mystic Seven. A common interest in the inner side of life will hold them together with greater strength than any association based on physically and materially oriented bonds. One will give strength to the other since no competition will exist. Decision making, however, will be left to the Seven.

TWO AND EIGHT

The Two must be prepared to be overshadowed by the Eight's protective and patriachal or matriachal attitudes. If this is done, a successful relationship in personal life and business can be established — the Eight as the outgoing, active provider and the Two as the busy supporter behind the scenes. The Eight will soon recognise and appreciate his or her dependence on the quiet strength of the Two.

TWO AND NINE

The Twos may suffer in personal relationships. Their demands for personal attention and other domestic obligations will not be met, as often as they desire, by the high-minded internationally oriented Nines. The Nines will find the Twos rather tiring and confining. For harmony to be maintained in personal relationships, the Twos will need to elevate their ideas and overcome self-interest.

A business association, however, can be successful without many personal adjustments. The Nines will come to depend on the Two's love of routine, method and detail.

TWO AND ELEVEN

Once again, the Twos will be overshadowed by the enthusiasm and zeal of the missionary Elevens. The psychic side of the Twos will appreciate the message of the Elevens but their speed may be just too much for the gentle and home-loving Twos.

TWO AND TWENTY-TWO

A good combination, where the straightforward Two will support the many-sided Twenty-two in a number of practical ways, especially in looking after routine but essential duties. The Twenty-Two will appreciate the value of the Two and use tact and encouragement to extract the best out of the Two. The Twos will, in turn, feel comforted and fulfilled in the service of the powerful Twenty-Two.

THREE AND ONE

Same as One and Three.

THREE AND TWO

Same as Two and Three.

THREE AND THREE

A life of excitement, social adventure and fulfilment of artistic talents is certain to follow the coalition of these extroverted and mentally active types. This will, however, portray only one side of the coin, as it were. On the other side, problems will rise involving the day-to-day functions of life. One will leave the responsibility to the other. Both parties will spend their money freely. Lack of planning and thought for the future will bring about circumstances that will place considerable pressure on this association. As both parties have free and independent natures neither will be prepared to assume a secondary role. Fundamentally a difficult association.

THREE AND FOUR

Immediate conflict can be expected from these basically different personalities. On the other hand, a partnership of exceptional balance and productivity can be developed if these basic differences are respected and used in a process of giving and taking. The Threes must appreciate the practicality of the Fours while understanding their lack of imagination. The Fours should take advantage of the Threes' creative ideas. If the Threes value the gifts of the Fours they will not find them tiresome. The Fours, in turn, should lift themselves up to appreciate the sense of humour and joy of living offered by the Threes.

A strong combination in business as well as in personal life can be established with strength in the foreground and background of activity if these basic adjustments are made.

THREE AND FIVE

A volatile combination. Constant verbal battles are inevitable. In spite of frequent differences of opinion, they will be drawn to each other by mutual interests in travel and the pursuit of pleasure, and particularly the mental challenges one will constantly hold out to the other. A productive combination in all forms of public entertainment. A third party will be needed to look after the practical aspects of life as these Threes and Fives will show no interest or capacity to look after routine and mundane responsibilities. They are both big spenders and money will go out as fast as it comes in. Both parties will be fond of gambling. A generally undesirable partnership from the point of view of domestic stability.

THREE AND SIX

In the domestic scene these two mentally oriented parties will find understanding sooner or later, but clashes may be expected initially. The outgoing ways of the society-loving Threes may be stifled by the home-loving Sixes. However, as both types are fond of entertainment — one outside the home and the other within the home — no great difficulties will be experienced in adjusting themselves to each other's tastes. Furthermore, a healthy and eager exchange of conversation and artistic interests will bring about a most enjoyable relationship.

Business associations, particularly in the entertainment and hospitality industries, can be very successful. The charm and initiative of the Threes will be guided by the logic and balance of the Sixes.

THREE AND SEVEN

In personal relationships a tremendous effort will be needed to form some degree of compatibility between these two different personality types. The talkative and extroverted Threes will not understand the contemplative and aloof Sevens. The Sevens, in turn, will not tolerate the constant chatter of the Threes or bother with their social needs and sentimental demands. Both parties will be scornful of each other's attitudes.

A successful business association, however, can be formed. The intuition and efficiency of the Sevens, particularly in financial affairs, and the charm and oral gifts of the Threes, can combine well to produce a profitable partnership. There will be a mutual recognition of each other's high intelligence though their thoughts are directed into different channels.

THREE AND EIGHT

Another combination that augurs trouble in personal relationships but which could produce a formidable partnership in business. In private life the Threes will find the Eights too authoritative and the Eights' dedication to work with little time left for "play" will leave the Threes high and dry. The Eights, for their part, will find their Three partners hard to keep up with. The social involvements of the Threes will be too much for the hard-working Eights. There will also be constant bickering over money matters. However, in business, each could occupy an area where maximum use can be made of each other's talents. The corporate power of the Eights and the agile minds of the Threes can combine to produce an extraordinary association.

THREE AND NINE

The quality of practicality will be conspicuous by its absence among these mentally oriented personalities. Excess of idealism and generosity will make this a poor business combination. However, a rich personal relationship can emerge from this association after an initial period of adaptation. As the ego of the Threes is very strong, and as the Nines have emerged out of self-centredness into wider perspectives, some adjustments will be needed, particularly on the part of the Threes. The Threes will need to lift themselves to the level of the Nines' internationalism. The Nines' compassion and understanding will encourage the Threes' efforts. The Threes' initial attempts to dominate the Nines will ultimately prove futile. Eventually, a fine association can be formed through their mutual interests in travel, the fine arts and other cultural activities.

THREE AND ELEVEN

Once again impracticality will be a problem. However, the Threes and Elevens will enjoy each other's company since both are compulsive talkers and will not run out of subjects on which to talk. There will be some opposition between the impersonal attitudes of the Elevens and the personal or ego-centred nature of the Threes. The creative and inventive abilities of both parties will be put to maximum advantage. The domestic side of life will be neglected as well as other mundane issues.

THREE AND TWENTY-TWO

An unlikely combination. If it does occur, the Threes will be overshadowed by the Twenty-twos. The Twenty-twos, in turn, will find the Threes immature. The Threes should expect to take a subordinate position. If this position is accepted the Threes will fulfil themselves since the Twenty-twos have the capacity to provide them with all the opportunity they need to do so.

FOUR AND ONE

Same as One and Four.

FOUR AND TWO

Same as Two and Four.

FOUR AND THREE

Same as Three and Four.

FOUR AND FOUR

Except for any differences in their background conditioning, there will be very little to be sorted out between these naturally compatible people. A partnership of tremendous strength can be formed since both parties will be working towards the same aims. There will be coalition instead of competition. Achievement in the business world or in private life is assured. They will enjoy much personal happiness and gain the respect of the community in which they live. The risk of gradually slipping into a groove in their style of living should be watched for and avoided. If this is allowed to happen it will be an unfortunate wastage of talents.

FOUR AND FIVE

A combination fraught with many difficulties. Fundamental adjustments will be needed before any harmony is enjoyed, especially in personal relationships. The Fours will find it hard to cope with the Fives' impulsiveness and constant desire for change and movement. The Fives, on the other hand, will not put up with the Fours' sober habits and will display fierce resentment towards the Fours' attempts to restrict their movements. Arguments regarding finances are certain to arise.

A successful business partnership can be formed with the Fours in charge of finances and production and the Fives taking over communication and selling.

FOUR AND SIX

A splendid combination in business as well as in private life. Finances will be safe in the hands of either party. Neither party will be inclined to take a gamble. Commonsense and logic will be the governing factors in all their dealings. In personal relationships their common love of home will hold them together. Both parties will be fond of the culinary arts and share the love of ease and other physical comforts. Their homes will vibrate with simplicity, hospitality and harmony.

FOUR AND SEVEN

A lasting association of any sort is assured with this pair. Each one will show high regard for the other's desire for perfection in whatever activity in which they engage: the Fours particularly in mechanics and technology, the Sevens in scientific and other intellectual pursuits. Their common ground will be love of the land. Financial stability is assured since both parties have an excellent money sense. The practicality of the Fours will combine well with the imagination and insight of the Sevens. Their family lives will be secure and harmonious.

More light-heartedness should be brought into this union. The stronger Fours may not always agree with the Sevens in their research into the metaphysical aspects of life, though they will respect the Sevens' need for fulfilment in this area.

FOUR AND EIGHT

One of the strongest possible partnerships in business. Both parties are commercially oriented — the Fours towards small to average size businesses and the Eights towards enterprises on a large scale. The combining of these two will lift the Fours nearer the limitless ambitions of the Eights, thus forming a powerful and resourceful partnership. The Fours will continue to look after the practical day-to-day responsibilities, while the Eights will use their entrepreneurial skills to constantly seek expansion of their undertakings.

Harmony will exist in private life as well. Both partners have the same ambitions, albeit on different levels. Almost immediate success in the material world will be the reward of their efforts and they will always have a healthy bank balance. However, both parties are likely to expose themselves to the danger of overwork.

FOUR AND NINE

As these are different types with well-established personalities of their own, one can learn a great deal from the other. The greatest gifts of the Fours, which the Nines lack, are common-sense, practicality, emotional stability and financial acumen. The Fours, in turn, can be introduced to the great wide world of travel and cultural activity under the influence of the Nines. The Fours will need to cooperate and not try to curtail the many outside interests of the Nines. They may support the Nines behind the scenes or join them in the foreground of activity. Either way, the Fours will benefit. The Nines will not be without gain either. If these adjustments are made through the practicality of the Fours and the wisdom of the Nines an outstanding association can be established.

FOUR AND ELEVEN

In a long-term personal relationship many adjustments will be required. The Fours will consider the Elevens merely talkers and dreamers. The pragmatic Fours will find it difficult to adjust to the idealism of the Elevens. The Elevens will experience extreme restlessness and constriction under the discipline of the Fours. Yet, in business they could profit by wise use of each other's talents. The inventive genius of the Elevens could be put to practical use and physical form by the Fours.

FOUR AND TWENTY-TWO

The internationalism and unlimited range of the outlook of the Twenty-twos may be a bit too much for the conservative Fours. There may be upsets in private life. The Fours' natural desire to settle down into a secure niche will not be fulfilled by the impersonal and active Twenty-twos. A business association could be much easier. The Twenty-two will need and come to depend on the loyalty and reliability of the Fours.

FIVE AND ONE

Same as One and Five.

FIVE AND TWO

Same as Two and Five.

FIVE AND THREE

Same as Three and Five.

FIVE AND FOUR

Same as Four and Five.

FIVE AND FIVE

A relationship in which close bonds will not be maintained. There will be no restraint on each other's freedom of movement. One will not attempt to pry into the other's life. Rare attempts to do so will result in dishonesty by both parties. The combination of these two impetuous types will lead to strife. Their domestic lives will be in disorder and so will the state of their finances. Both will enjoy a streak of "luck" in gambling but money is likely to go out faster than it comes in. One party will constantly attempt to shift the responsibility of mundane duties on to the other. Either separately or together, they will be constantly on the move. Although considerable initial excitement will be enjoyed, the association will inevitably come to an early termination.

FIVE AND SIX

In domestic life a great deal of hard work will be required for a meaningful relationship to be achieved. The Fives' restlessness and impulsiveness will constantly clash with the Sixes' attachment to home and domestic responsibilities. The Fives may often leave the Sixes "carrying the baby", so to speak. Frequent absences from home by the Fives will generate suspicion and jealousy on the part of the Sixes. The Fives will not be able to cope with the restrictions the Sixes will attempt to impose on them. If the Fives could contain their restlessness and accept their share of domestic responsibility, this pair could join in and enjoy much social activity. In business life many of these problems will not arise and a profitable association can be formed.

FIVE AND SEVEN

In private life this partnership will be incompatible. The tension and intense activity of the Fives will upset the Sevens' search for quietude and privacy. The natural curiosity of the Fives will make troublesome inroads into the Sevens' love of privacy. The Fives will feel left out of the Sevens' company and their hurried attempts to gain entry into the contemplative world of the Sevens will only drive the latter further into themselves. The Fives will not be able to respect the needs of the Sevens. The Sevens for their part will find the Fives much too noisy, emotional and unreliable. They will, however, appreciate the Fives' versatility and alert and active minds and tolerate them up to a point. They can become good friends and acquaintances because the Fives' high spirits will lift the Sevens out of their customary seriousness.

Mutual respect for each other's intelligence and expertise in their own areas will make this a good business partnership — the Fives being the front people and the Sevens active in the background.

FIVE AND EIGHT

Another difficult combination in personal relationships. Emotional control will be a grave problem. Also, one will try to run the life of the other. The Fives will find the Eights too conservative, while the Eights will charge the Fives with irresponsibility. If the two meet each other halfway a profitable relationship can be formed. The versatility of the Fives will be of inestimable value to the schemes of the Eights. The judgement of the Eights will act as a buffer to the impetuosity of the Fives.

This can be turned into a lucrative business association with the Eights building and producing and the Fives buying and selling. Domestic life will be a low priority. The little time left after business affairs will be spent on travel and social obligations.

FIVE AND NINE

A happy combination. Both parties have open minds and are able to adjust to changing circumstances without effort. Love of travel and a natural curiosity will be a strong common bond. Once again the Fives' great versatility will be of real help to the idealistic and impractical Nines. The Nines' wisdom will guide the volatile Fives. This pair can gather an enormous amount of experience in life. They will not be without friction, however. Both are emotional — the Fives constantly displaying their emotions and the Nines bottling them up and erupting from time to time.

This is not a strong business combination. Neither party is really business-minded. Human relationships and worldly experience are more important. The domestic side of life will, on the other hand, be of little importance. Very little time will be spent at home.

FIVE AND ELEVEN

An unproductive combination. There will be much talk and little performance. They will enjoy each other's company and will exchange ideas freely. The Fives, who have a much greater need for physical experience, will find the Elevens rather high-minded, while the Elevens will accuse the Fives of immaturity.

FIVE AND TWENTY-TWO

The versatility of the Fives will once again be harnessed by the practical Twenty-twos, especially in business. In private life the mature Twenty-twos will find the attitudes of the Fives somewhat juvenile. The Fives will need to submit to the superior wisdom of the Twenty-twos.

SIX AND ONE

Same as One and Six.

SIX AND TWO

Same as Two and Six.

SIX AND THREE

Same as Three and Six.

SIX AND FOUR
Same as Four and Six.

SIX AND FIVE
Same as Five and Six.

SIX AND SIX
This will be a partnership of deep tranquillity with home as the centre of all activity. Partners will experience much happiness in jointly beautifying their homes, spending much time in them and participating in innumerable common interests. No form of competition will enter here. A life of comfort, enjoyed at an easy pace, will be preferred to the competitive rat-race to satisfy high ambitions. These people will be well known for their old-fashioned hospitality; however, those who need a faster and more exciting form of entertainment will find these Sixes somewhat dull.

A business association will show lack of enterprise and the absence of a strong competitive spirit.

SIX AND SEVEN
Both partners are home based, but the home may be a place of accord as well as discord. They could be "at sixes and sevens" in their ideas of home. The Sixes' natural hospitality and customary use of the home for entertainment will not be shared by the Sevens who will prefer their home to be a sanctuary for privacy. Home maintenance will not cause problems since the Sixes will have full run of the house while the Sevens will take charge of the garden. The Sixes' need for conversation will not be met by the taciturn Sevens. Both parties are subject to forms of melancholy. The Sixes' desire for social service will not be shared by the recluse Sevens.

Despite these apparent basic differences a very meaningful and lasting partnership can be established if these people understand each other's genuine needs. The Sixes' spiritual needs will be met by the Sevens, while the Sevens will find that all domestic chores will be looked after by their partners.

A good business combination. Success will be achieved through sound financial knowledge and a reputation for honesty and responsibility.

SIX AND EIGHT

One of the strongest combinations in the domestic scene. The Sixes will provide all the support in the home, while the Eights build a career in business or public service. There will be no competition here. Each will support the other by performing well in the other's departments of activity. Their homes will be showpieces of affluence. The community will also benefit from this type of partnership through the social service of the Sixes and the philanthrophy of the Eights.

Business associations will be equally successful.

SIX AND NINE

A natural attraction exists between these people, promising a most compatible union in personal life. A deep and abiding friendship will automatically develop. There will be agreement on almost all aspects of living. Their aims will be the same. Selfishness will not enter here. Each one will bring out the best in the other. Both parties are humanitarians dedicated to self-less service, from which a great deal of happiness will be derived. They will also be jointly dedicated to the pursuit of a genteel and refined way of life.

There will be no lack of support for each other in business life either. However, neither party will be strongly business-minded. Businesses dealing with the relief of human suffering will attract these people.

SIX AND ELEVEN

Another good combination. Both parties are idealists and will be able to communicate on a mental level and satisfy each other's need for oral expression. Both are dedicated to a peaceful way of life, though the Elevens can be spirited and explosive when they allow themselves to be carried away by their inspirations. The Sixes will see that the domestic responsibilities are not neglected while the Elevens will offer wider perspectives and greater opportunities for motivation.

A good business partnership. The Sixes' excellent money sense and the Elevens' inventiveness can work successfuly together.

SIX AND TWENTY-TWO

Another association where harmony will prevail, provided the Sixes are prepared to assume the greater portion of domestic responsibilities and allow the Twenty-twos freedom of action. Common ground will be found in humanitarian works and social involvement.

A good business arrangement. Mutual trust, responsibility and honesty will contribute to form a strong association.

SEVEN AND ONE

Same as One and Seven.

SEVEN AND TWO

Same as Two and Seven.

SEVEN AND THREE

Same as Three and Seven.

SEVEN AND FOUR

Same as Four and Seven.

SEVEN AND FIVE

Same as Five and Seven.

SEVEN AND SIX

Same as Six and Seven.

SEVEN AND SEVEN

Many unusual features will arise from this combination. Each will be intuitively aware of the other's needs. Very little oral communication will take place, nor will there be demonstration of emotion. A strong bond will be forged through their mutual interest in study, the love of nature and a recluse or semi-recluse way of life. They will be oblivious of the common issues that normally absorb the attention of the average person. The pair will soon gain a reputation for unapproachability. Pettiness will not enter this relationship. Both parties may suffer from dreaminess and melancholy, the latter being brought about by frustration because of pressures from the outside world. They will be content to live in an inner world of their own and will always resent and reject any intrusions.

A good business combination, provided selling and public relations are not involved.

SEVEN AND EIGHT

A business partnership of considerable profit and strength can be formed between these two. The Sevens' natural flair for wise investment and other money dealings will combine well with the Eights' business and executive talents. The Eights will find the Sevens scrupulously honest and entirely dependable, while the Sevens will be more than content to work within the business network built up by the Eights.

Personal relationships will be difficult. The spiritually oriented Sevens, who can detach themselves from their material possessions, will not be happy with the worldly Eights whose measure of success is determined by power and wealth.

The Sevens' aloofness will upset the Eights who will expect support and cooperation in their affairs. The pair will find it difficult to meet on common ground. The Eights will need to respect the Sevens' need for seclusion and individuality and any attempts by them to organise the lives of the Sevens will only drive the latter further into themselves. The assertive habits adopted by the Eights in business should not be used in the domestic scene.

SEVEN AND NINE

A relationship of great fulfilment can be developed here once the natural tendencies of each party are understood and accepted. Their common ground will be the accumulation of worthwhile knowledge and spiritual unfoldment, and no closer bond can exist than this joint venture into the realms of metaphysics. However, the Sevens will want to remain within these realms of inquiry with no desire to transform their knowledge into the world of activity. The Nines on the other hand will feel the urge to preach and find practical ways to apply the knowledge and wisdom they have gained. Reconciliation is needed between these two attitudes.

On a more day-to-day level, the soft-spoken and aloof

Sevens will accept the Nines' ability to communicate ideas. More importantly, the Sevens, who are the most intolerant of all loud-spoken and abrasive individuals, will respect the superior quality of the Nines' speech and well-informed minds.

SEVEN AND ELEVEN

The Sevens will agree with much of the idealism of the Elevens but will not go beyond mental acceptance. They will not be seen with the Elevens on the same platform. The methods of the Elevens will not be to their liking. The Sevens are able to see through the impracticality of many of the Elevens' schemes. However, when the Elevens function on a scientific level, they will find support from the Sevens. Common ground is found here. The Elevens should take care not to talk excessively with their Seven partners.

SEVEN AND TWENTY-TWO

The Sevens may find it tiresome to keep up with the many activities of the Twenty-twos. They will resent demands made upon their time, especially if public appearances are involved. If this problem is overcome, mutual respect for each other's spiritual awareness combined with practicality will hold them together in a worthwhile relationship.

EIGHT AND ONE

Same as One and Eight.

EIGHT AND TWO

Same as Two and Eight.

EIGHT AND THREE

Same as Three and Eight.

EIGHT AND FOUR

Same as Four and Eight.

EIGHT AND FIVE

Same as Five and Eight.

EIGHT AND SIX
Same as Six and Eight.

EIGHT AND SEVEN
Same as Seven and Eight.

EIGHT AND EIGHT
Mutual recognition of each other's talents and resultant coalition of power will make this a formidable partnership in business. It is this type of combination that is able to sweep aside all forms of competition.

In personal affairs the situation may be complicated. Without the common aim of business success, two authoritative and organised people will want to gain ascendency over each other. This contest will be unconscious and if its futility is recognised at the early stages and a policy of cooperation adopted, another powerful union can be formed. Both parties are sensitive and their feelings are easily hurt. Emotional turmoil will do much damage to an intimate relationship and this too must be closely watched.

EIGHT AND NINE
Another good combination in business. The wider perspectives of the Nines will enhance the high ambitions of the Eights. The invaluable asset of the Nines' ambassadorial talents will be put to maximum use.

In private life the Eights will seek to control the Nines. They will not be pleased with the Nines' generosity, impressionability and unbusinesslike way. The Nines on the other hand will begrudge the amount of time the Eights spend at work. Also, the Eights' lack of interest in social, cultural and spiritual matters will disturb the Nines. However, the high sense of justice of the Eights and the wisdom of the Nines can combine to overcome these basic differences. If both parties work towards the success of their relationship, accomplishment rather than failure will be the result.

EIGHT AND ELEVEN
While the Eights hold control over the running of a business, the inventive and inspirational side of the Elevens will be used pro-

fitably by the practical Eights. In domestic life and other personal relationships the Eights will be intolerant towards the Elevens' impracticality, idealism and indifference to financial gain. The Elevens will naturally resent what they will regard as materialistic attitudes in the Eights and their lack of interest in abstract matters.

EIGHT AND TWENTY-TWO

An association here can turn out to be outstanding in both business and personal life. A few personality problems will have to be overcome, however, before success is achieved. The superior Twenty-twos will have the capacity to make the correct overtures and handle the assertive Eights. The Eights, in turn, will not fail to respect the exceptional talents of their Twenty-two associates and loved ones.

NINE AND ONE

Same as One and Nine.

NINE AND TWO

Same as Two and Nine.

NINE AND THREE

Same as Three and Nine.

NINE AND FOUR

Same as Four and Nine.

NINE AND FIVE

Same as Five and Nine.

NINE AND SIX

Same as Six and Nine.

NINE AND SEVEN

Same as Seven and Nine.

NINE AND EIGHT
Same as Eight and Nine.

NINE AND NINE
Two Nines can form an association providing unlimited scope for expression of wide-ranging interests in human relations. Co-existence will be easy and enriched by mutual cooperation in all their joint ventures. There will however be an occasional outburst of anger leading to critical exchange of words between the two. These outbursts will usually be brief and will not damage the relationship. Association on a personal level will be more profitable than on a business level, though the two can combine well in administration and organisation at executive levels in government service and large business concerns.

NINE AND ELEVEN
The visionary outlook of these parties may bring them together, but not necessarily hold them together, unless they try to be more practical and down-to-earth. Too much idealism and too little practicality will be the problem here. The domestic side of life will be neglected. A successful business partnership is unlikely since neither party will be interested in buying and selling and in other aspects of commercial and industrial life.

NINE AND TWENTY-TWO
A good business association can be formed, with the Twenty-twos bringing practical application into the partnership. The Nines will provide expertise in public relations. In family life, the down-to-earth Twenty-twos may find the mentally oriented Nines overgenerous and restless. In spite of these differences, an association of considerable benefit to themselves and many others can be formed without much difficulty.

ELEVEN AND ELEVEN
A lively combination that will be full of mutual interest in abstract thought. A constant exchange of ideas will take place. The inventiveness of the Elevens, if brought out and combined, will see an association of great productivity.

ELEVEN AND TWENTY-TWO

A most desirable association in both business and personal affairs. One will complement the other perfectly. The inventiveness, idealism and power of speech of the Elevens will merge easily with the practicality and humanitarianism of the Twenty-twos.

TWENTY-TWO AND TWENTY-TWO

A combination rarely found. The merger of these two very powerful persons could lead to competition resulting in frustration or, alternatively, a coalition of power leading to unlimited potential for enterprise.

Irrigators canalize the waters,
Fletchers bend the arrows,
Carpenters carve the wood,
Wise men fashion themselves.

THE DHAMMAPADA

FEMALE NAMES LIST

Vibration Number 1 Names

—A—

Adalia
Adaline
Adelina
Agnes
Aileen
Ailene
Aleen
Alene
Aleria
Alina
Alise
Alix
Allison
Allyn
Amalee
Amalia
Amie
Andi
Angelique
Anica
Annice
Arleen
Arlene
Arliene
Ashlan
Ashlea
Astrea
Athalla
Aurea
Avaline
Aviva

—B—

Babe
Beitris
Bel
Bergette
Bernelle
Bertine
Bethesda
Bonnibel
Brandy
Breanna
Breeanne
Brieanna
Brittany
Bryar
Brynie

—C—

Cristal
Calanthe
Calli
Cameo
Camille
Cammy
Carina
Carley
Carlita
Carlyn
Carolina
Cathie
Cazanne
Chanara
Charelle
Charisse
Chenoa
Cherey
Cindy
Cirilla
Cissie
Clarissa
Clarita
Claudette
Cora
Corabelle
Coretta
Corine
Crystina

—D—

Dalveena
Daneele
Danett
Dani
Daniela
Daughn
Davine
Delfine
Delora
Delphine

Dian
Dina
Domenica
Dorelia
Dottie
Dove

—E—

Ebonee
Eda
Eden
Edith
Edrine
Elaine
Eldora
Electra
Elena
Elfrida
Elinor
Elisa
Elisia
Ellwyn
Elsa
Emily
Erma
Ernestine
Eva
Evaleen

—F—

Fabia
Faye
Fayette
Fellon
Freya

—G—

Gabi
Georgianna
Gerry
Gertie

Gillian
Glenys
Glynnis

—H—

Hannah
Harrietta
Heloise
Henrietta
Hilary
Hildegarde
Honi

—I—

Ilana
Iliana
India
Ira
Iris
Irmina

—J—

Jabina
Jamila
Janella
Janey
Jasmyn
Jaya
Jayne
Joanna
Joceline
Julita

—K—

Kalila
Kalla
Kallee
Kandy
Kate
Katherine

Katie
Kay
Kaylene
Kerryn
Kimberley
Kirstin
Kyra

—L—

Lacey
Lainne
Lalita
Lana
Larina
Larrae
Lashae
Leanda
Leisa
Leitha
Lenise
Lenna
Lesa
Letizia
Letty
Levana
Lewise
Lexie
Liana
Lianne
Lois
Lonie
Lora
Loree
Loren
Loretta
Lorinda
Lorine
Loris
Louanne
Lucine
Lurline

—M—

Madelaine
Madelon
Mae
Maggi
Maida
Maire
Malena
Mandie
Mangena
Maraline
Marette
Margy
Marie
Marjory
Marlena
Marni
Maryanne
Mavis
Medea
Meggie
Melesa
Melisse
Meredith
Meris
Merola
Meryl
Mikhala
Mina
Minerva
Minnie
Mirna
Monica
Moriah
Murita

—N—

Nance
Nancie
Nanice
Narilia
Narrila

Narrilia
Natahlya
Natasha
Nedda
Neroli
Nerroli
Nettie
Neysa

—O—

Odelia
Odelinda
Ornice

—P—

Pat
Patreece
Patty
Philine
Philly
Pru

—Q—

Quinta

—R—

Rachelle

Raegan
Ranica
Rebecca
Ree
Reeve
Reiva
Rhoda
Ria
Ronice
Rosanna
Roseanne
Roxanne
Rozyte

—S—

Sabene
Sabina
Sabrina
Selia
Selinda
Seton
Shantell
Shari
Sharmin
Shauna
Shehan
Sherida
Shira
Sibelle
Sibilla

Stacey
Stephie
Susette
Susie
Suzanne
Suzy
Sydelle

—T—

Taladwyn
Tamika
Tanarra
Tanille
Taylor
Tennille
Tessa
Tyahne
Tyne
Tyra

—U—

Ulla

—V—

Valore
Vera
Verine
Vivienne

—W—

Wendeline
Wendi

—Y—

Yasmeen
Yolanthe
Yona
Ysabel

—Z—

Zahara
Zandra
Zanette
Zara
Zaria
Zenia
Zoe

Vibration Number 2 Names

—A—

Abagael
Addrenia
Adina
Ador
Adrea
Agatha

Ainslee
Akyra
Alana
Aleasha
Alesia
Aletha
Alfreda
Alithea

Allegra
Althea
Alvita
Analia
Andree
Andria
Anelina
Anette

Ann
Anni
Antoinetta
Antonia
April
Ara
Ardeen
Ardene

Ardeth
Arlana
Arly
Artinka
Asha
Audey
Audrey
Aurora
Avalon

—B—

Beata
Bedelia
Bela
Belia
Belinda
Beneta
Berneta
Bernice
Bev
Beverlee
Biancha
Bianka
Bridget
Bridie
Brigit
Briony

—C—

Caitrin
Calista
Calla
Caresa
Carilla
Carlynne
Carmita
Cassie
Cate
Catherine
Catie
Catrin
Celestine

Celinica
Chaney
Christina
Claudina
Corabel
Corena
Coriss
Correna
Cosetta
Cristin
Cyra

—D—

Daisie
Damara
Damaris
Damon
Dana
D'anne
Daph
Dasie
Dayle
Deandra
Dearne
Debby
Delys
Denise
Denna
Deon
Desiree
Devora
Diana
Dianne
Dione
Dora
Doretta
Doris
Dylan

—E—

Eadith
Edrena

Edwardine
Edwina
Eirene
Elenore
Elissa
Elita
Ellessandra
Elli
Elnora
Eloise
Elyn
Emlynn
Emmalyn
Emmy
Erina
Estella
Estrella
Evelyn
Evon
Ewa

—F—

Fabrienne
Fanya
Farica
Fayina
Faythe
Florrie

—G—

Gail
Garnet
Gaye
Gayelene
Gilly
Gwendolyn
Gypsy

—H—

Hanna
Hatty

Heather
Helyna
Holli

—I—

Idelle
Ines
Irena
Irisa
Isa
Isabelle
Ivana
Ivy

—J—

Jaclyn
Jade
Jaime
Jamie
Jannel
Jeni
Jessamy
Jilana
Jileena
Jodi
Joline
Jordi
Josephine
Josselyn
Judye

—K—

Kacie
Kaelah
Kandice
Karlie
Kathy
Katrina
Kaya
Kaytlin
Keddie

Kelly
Kelsi
Kerrilee
Ketti
Kirby
Kiri
Kittie
Kristian
Kristina

—L—

Leitia
Lellani
Lenora
Leta
Lewana
Linnelle
Liz
Lorena
Lorraine
Lucille
Lurette
Lynda
Lynette
Lynn
Lyra

—M—

Maddy
Madelyn
Maisie
Maleesa
Malissa
Marcella
Margaret
Margarite
Margot
Marian
Marilyn
Marina
Marje
Marjie

Marlyn
Marna
Martez
Masie
Melessa
Melloney
Melody
Merrille
Midge
Mildred
Mileeta
Mindy
Mirelle
Miriana
Missie
Modesty
Moira
Morganna
Moyanna
Murial
Mylene

—N—

Nada
Nadia
Nadine
Nan
Narida
Neisha
Nerine
Neryl
Nevada
Nina
Ninnette
Nizana
Noleen
Nolene
Norah

—O—

Odetta
Olisa

Oralia
Orlena
Othilia

—P—

Page
Paige
Patsi
Pauleen
Paulina
Penny
Penrose
Perle
Petrina
Phalen
Phenica
Phenicia
Pollyanna

—R—

Rachel
Rainie
Rakel
Raquel
Reina
Rena
Renee
Rheannin
Rhianna
Rikah
Riki
Risa
Robyn
Roda
Rolanda
Roma
Rosalind
Rozene
Rozina
Rubina

—S—

Sadie
Sandi
Sarah
Sari
Selena
Shaine
Shara
Sharai
Sharne
Sheelagh
Shelli
Shereen
Sibel
Sommer
Sonya
Steffi
Stephani
Susan

—T—

Taleah
Tameeka
Tammi
Tamsyn
Taya
Tracie
Trish
Tyann

—U—

Ursula
Ursuline
Utina

—V—

Valenaine
Valissa
Valli
Valonia

Vania
Varina
Verena
Violet

—W—

Wenda
Winnie
Winola

—Z—

Zanther
Zita
Zonia

Zorina
Zuri

Vibration Number 3 Names

—A—

Aasha
Abby
Abilene
Acandy
Acantha
Adelice
Adelle
Adora
Adoree
Adriana
Agneta
Albina
Alejandra
Aleta
Alexina
Alice
Alleysia
Allie
Alya
Amber
Amy
Anna
Annabelle
Annalise
Anneliese
Annis
Annmarie
Ardelle
Ariane
Arlyne
Aurel

—B—

Barby
Beatrisa
Belisia
Bethany
Bettine
Bianca
Blisse
Bobbi
Branca
Brandi
Bree
Bren
Bretta
Biar
Brietta
Bronwyn
Bronya
Brooke

—C—

Caitlyn
Calida
Camila
Cammi
Candice
Caressa
Carlie
Carlin
Catharina
Cathy

Cecily
Celia
Celinda
Celisha
Channel
Charity
Charleen
Charlene
Charlotte
Chauntel
Chere
Cherie
Chloris
Chris
Christelle
Cissy
Claire
Clare
Clarette
Clarrette
Clea
Clio
Clover
Colleen
Corallie
Corella
Corey
Corissa
Cresta
Cynthie

—D—

Dalila
Dannae
Daphne
Darelle
Darrelle
Davita
Deanna
Debra
Dehlia
Deonne
Dollie
Donna
Dorena
Dot
Dotty

—E—

Eleanore
Elica
Ella
Ellen
Ellsabeth
Elrica
Elyse
Emmalynne
Essie
Esther
Eugenie
Eunice
Evanna

Evita
Evonne
Eyde

—F—

Fae
Fayanne
Ferne
Fifi
Fran
Frances

—G—

Gemma
Georgette
Georgie
Geraldine
Geri
Gerri
Gisele
Griselda
Gwyneth

—H—

Hayleigh
Heddi
Henrika
Hester

—I—

Ianthe
Illeen
Iona
Irita
Isidora

—J—

Jacalyn
Jackie

Jacintha
Jacquette
Jamina
Jane
Janette
Janida
Janie
Jann
Janyte
Jean
Jenee
Jennie
Jessica
Jocelyn
Jodee
Joelene
Joni
Julie
Juliette
Junella

—K—

Kandi
Karlea
Karlene
Kerrie
Kira
Kirra
Kristelle
Kristiana
Kristy

—L—

Lahela
Laney
Laurette
Laurie
Leila
Lenice
Leonore
Lilian
Linsey

Lisbeth
Lorey
Lorita
Lynaire

—M—

Madella
Madge
Mandy
Maralyn
Mariana
Marianne
Marielle
Marilla
Marquette
Mary
Maud
Maxine
May
Maybelle
Meggy
Meghan
Meridel
Merissa
Merl
Merolyn
Merril
Merryn
Micala
Mollie
Morena
Myra
Myrtle

—N—

Nadeene
Nancy
Nanine
Natassia
Nathalia
Nellie
Netty

Norine
Norra

—O—

Olethea
Omena
Ondina
Ophelia

—P—

Pam
Pamela
Pammie
Pascale
Patti
Peri
Perri
Phaidra
Prudy

—Q—

Quenby

—R—

Rachael
Raelyn
Ranna
Reanne
Rhiannon
Rita
Rohana
Romaine
Rona
Rosalia
Rosaline
Rose
Rozelle
Ruby

—S—

Sandra
Sara
Sarine
Sarsha
Sasha
Shanan
Sharon
Shaylee
Shevonne
Shey
Shirl
Shona
Sibylle
Simone
Sirena
Stace
Stacie
Sunny
Susana
Susanne
Susy
Sybille

—T—

Taegan
Tai
Talene
Tamazin
Temiria
Terrie
Tonya
Trisha
Trudey
Tyissa

—U—

Ursel

—V—

Valentia
Vilma
Vivyan
Voleta

—W—

Willetta
Winnifred
Winonah
Wyuna

—X—

Ximena

—Y—

Yonita
Yovila

—Z—

Zelda
Zofia
Zorana

Vibration Number 4 Names

—A—

Abra
Adel
Adelind
Adyth
Afina
Ainsley
Alarice
Alayne
Alecia
Alessandra
Aleyna
Alleen
Allina
Allix
Allyce
Alvie
Alysia
Alyss
Amberly
Anastasia
Andreana
Anet
Angela
Annabel
Anthea
Ardyth
Ariella
Astred
Athena
Athenia
Audie
Audre
Audrie
Aurelia
Averil

—B—

Belikia
Belita
Bell
Bena
Benedetta
Benne
Bernadette
Bernetta
Berthe
Beryle
Betica
Beverley
Billie
Blanch
Blyth
Breahna
Breehannah
Brigid
Brit
Brylee

—C—

Cade
Calley
Candace
Candi
Caralie
Careece
Cari
Carleen
Carlene
Carlina
Carol
Cassy
Caty
Cecily
Celestyn
Charmain
Charyl
Chiara
Chrissi
Christel
Cindee
Cindia
Cira
Cloris
Constance

Coral
Cordelia
Courtney
Cree
Cristobel

—D—

Dacie
Dael
Daile
Daisy
Dallas
Danella
Darice
Darwyn
Dela
Delia
Denice
Denys
Devi
Di
Doanna
Doralyne
Dorella
Dyane
Dyann

—E—

Echo
Edythe
Effie
Elin
Ellean
Ellena
Elmira
Elspeth
Elva
Elvira
Emelda
Emelin
Emilia
Emiline

Enrika

—F—

Faina
Felice
Ferdinanda
Fleurette

—G—

Gae
Gene
Genette
Genevieve
Genni
Georgina
Germain
Gill
Gilli
Gina
Gipsy
Gizelle
Glady
Glyn
Gwen

—H—

Haila
Hayley
Hedda
Heidie
Helene
Helouise
Hettie
Honey

—I—

Idelia
Iline
Ilyssa
Isabeau

Isadora

—J—

Jacinta
Jacquenette
Janae
Janina
Janna
Jeanine
Jeanne
Jensine
Jesse
Jessie
Jewell
Jillian
Joan
Johtie
Jonine
Josie
Joyce
Juanita
Judie
Julina
Juniata
Justina

—K—

Kara
Karen
Karinda
Karlana
Karoline
Karly
Karra
Kathi
Kathleen
Kathlene
Kaylah
Kendrea
Kerene
Kiandra
Kiara

Kitty
Kristel
Krysta
Kyla
Kylee
Kym

—L—

Lachelle
Lari
Launnie
Laureen
Laurene
Laureth
Lealia
Lee
Leontine
Letitia
Lia
Lily
Linda
Linette
Llianne
Lola
Lorelie
Louine
Luana
Luanne

—M—

Manuela
Marcie
Marice
Mariel
Marieta
Marilin
Marinka
Marjy
Martina
Marya
Marys
Megan

Melinda
Melisah
Mercia
Merline
Michelle
Missy
Monique
Musette

—N—

Narelle
Narilla
Narrilla
Natala
Nerissa
Nessa
Nicole
Nicolette
Noelyn
Noleta
Novelle
Nyree

—O—

Odella
Oriana

—P—

Paulyne

Penni
Perrine
Phillis
Priscell

—Q—

Queenie

—R—

Raissa
Raye
Regine
Rikki
Roana
Roanne
Romona
Rosemarie
Rosene
Rosina
Roslyn
Rowena
Ruth
Ruthi

—S—

Sachi
Sadelle
Sallie
Sarena

Shaye
Sherry
Shirlee
Sofi
Sonia
Sophi
Star
Summa
Sybil
Sylvana

—T—

Tamerra
Tandra
Tara
Tasha
Teare
Theresa
Toni
Tracy
Trixie

—U—

Undine
Uria

—V—

Valda
Vale

Valencia
Varlie
Veleda
Venetia
Vi
Vivyanne

—W—

Wendye
Wilma
Winona
Winny

—X—

Xylina

—Y—

Yani
Yanvie
Yolande

—Z—

Zaneita
Zaneta
Zsofia
Zuleika

Vibration Number 5 Names

—A—

Abbi
Abigail
Acandi
Adah
Adahbelle
Adalie

Adela
Adelaide
Adelia
Adeline
Adi
Aila
Airlia
Alberta

Aldea
Aleda
Aleida
Aletta
Aline
Alisha
Allana
Ally

Aloyse
Alsha
Alvina
Alvinia
Alyssa
Alzena
Amelia
Amelinda

Amity
Annalice
Annika
Anya
Ardelia
Aretina
Arline
Ashla
Ashlee
Ashlen
Asta
Astra
Auburn
Aura
Auria

—B—

Bab
Bella
Bellanca
Bergitte
Bessie
Bethea
Birgitta
Bonnie
Breanne
Brigida
Brigitta
Brita
Bryni

—C—

Caitlin
Candis
Cara
Caren
Carine
Carly
Carmill
Caroline
Caryl
Cathi

Cathleen
Cathlene
Cazbah
Celestyna
Celka
Cerise
Chanea
Charnea
Chelsey
Chenara
Cherry
Clarisse
Clymene
Coraline
Corette
Corie
Cornelia
Corrie
Cristel
Crystine

—D—

Dalene
Danica
Darby
Dareece
Dari
Darleen
Darlene
Debbee
Dee
Delaine
Delisia
Deva
Dolly
Dominica
Dorothea
Dotti
Duana
Dyanna

—E—

Edie
Eileen
Eleisha
Elise
Ellyn
Elodie
Else
Elsie
Elyce
Emalia
Emelina
Emma
Emmalina
Enid
Enrica
Erlina
Essy
Ethel
Ettie
Eve
Evie
Ezra

—F—

Faustine
Fay
Fionna

—G—

Gayle
Genna
Gerti
Gladys
Glynis
Glynne

—H—

Haidee
Harrie

Harriette
Henriette
Hermina
Herminia
Hortense

—I—

Ida
Idalina
Imogene
Irma
Irmine
Isla

—J—

Jackalyn
Jacky
Jacoba
Jacobine
Jamay
Janelle
Janet
Jaril
Jasisa
Jaydine
Jaye
Jemimah
Jennelle
Jenny
Jillana
Joanne
Jocelin
Joelle
Joy
June

—K—

Kallie
Kanene
Karena
Kayla

Kaylee
Kellia
Kelsey
Kerry
Kirbee
Kirsti
Kristi
Kyleigh

—L—

Laine
Lainie
Lanette
Lanie
Lanni
Lara
Larine
Laryssa
Laverne
Lavinia
Lawrie
Leigh
Lelitia
Lena
Leticia
Libby
Lisa
Loni
Lorie
Louisa
Lucette
Lucrezia
Lyndal

—M—

Madelene
Magena
Mahira
Mair
Mairi
Malina
Mame

Mandi
Mariah
Marleen
Marlene
Maryann
Mathilda
Maureen
Maurene
Maurise
Meggi
Melanie
Melisa
Melleta
Melodee
Meridith
Merrin
Mia
Minda
Mira
Misty
Molly
Morgan
Moyna
Murielle

—N—

Nalda
Nalini
Nanci
Naydeen
Nelia
Nesta
Nicolina
Niles
Norella

—O—

Odele
Odelette
Odilia
Olivia
Onella

—P—

Pammy
Patricia
Phillane
Piaf
Primrose
Priscellia
Prissie
Prudence
Pruddie
Prudi
Pryde

—R—

Rayna
Rebekah
Rechelle
Renata
Rhea
Rhian
Rhyannan
Ricki
Riva
Romany
Rosalyn
Rosanne
Roseann
Rosslyn
Rozalin
Ryora

—S—

Sabine
Sabra
Sacha
Sal
Samantha
Sarita
Serilda
Sharlee
Shasta

Shayna
Shelley
Sher
Siobhan
Sofia
Sophia
Stacy
Steph
Stephi
Susi
Sybila

—T—

Tamasin
Tammatha
Teresa
Terry
Thelma
Tonia
Trilby
Tristi
Trudie

—U—

Udelle

—V—

Valera
Vallonia
Veda
Vedia
Vee
Velvet
Vere
Veronika
Violetta
Vivian

—W—

Whitney

—*Y*—

Yana
Yania

Yesmina
Yvanna
Yvonne

—*Z*—

Zada
Zarie

Zea
Zera
Zina
Zorah

Vibration Number 6 Names

—*A*—

Abagail
Ada
Ademine
Adria
Aida
Ailsa
Aimee
Ainslie
Alaine
Alanda
Alane
Alannah
Aldora
Alena
Aliane
Alisa
Alithia
Alleta
Allwyn
Altheda
Althee
Amalea
Andie
Aneline
Anett
Angelika
Antoinette
Ardine
Arette
Arlena
Ashleigh
Ashton
Atissa
Atlanta

Audry
Ava
Avis

—*B*—

Barbra
Belva
Belvia
Benita
Bertina
Betrix
Beverlie
Bobette
Bryna

—*C*—

Calantha
Camilla
Carlynn
Caron
Casia
Cass
Cathee
Cati
Cecilia
Celeste
Charissa
Charita
Chastity
Chrissandra
Christine
Clareta
Clarice
Claudetta

Claudia
Claudine
Connie
Corene
Corina
Corinne
Correne
Corrina
Corrinne
Cybil
Cyn

—*D*—

Dacy
Danette
Dara
Daria
Darien
D'Arne
Dasi
Davina
Dawn
Delilah
Delores
Delta
Dena
Desma
Devon
Diandra
Disa
Dixie
Dorette
Dorothy
Drusilla

—*E*—

Eadie
Earlene
Edina
Edlyn
Edna
Eira
Elana
Elinore
Emalaine
Emlyn
Emmelyn
Ernaline
Esme
Esmeralda
Estelle

—*F*—

Fabian
Fabriene
Fairlie
Fallon
Fanny
Fayth
Flavia
Flo
Florence
Fraya
Frederica

—*G*—

Gabie
Gay

Gaylene
Gerta
Gilda
Gilvia
Ginger
Ginny
Giselle
Gladdie
Greta
Gwyn

—H—

Hailey
Halona
Heath
Helga
Hermoine

—I—

Ileana
Ilka
Ilona
Irene

—J—

Jacinda
Jacklin
Jami
Janel
Janice
Jantina
Jaynee
Jeri
Jerri
Jessalyn
Jessemy
Jessy
Jolette
Judy

—K—

Kahla
Kahlia
Kali
Karissa
Karolyn
Karryn
Karyn
Katia
Kaye
Kelleigh
Kendel
Kerstin
Khalia
Kim
Kirilee
Kirrilly
Kirsten
Klarysa
Kobie
Krista
Kristen
Kristine
Kymberlee
Kyna

—L—

Lanna
Laraine
Larena
Lark
Latecia
Laurel
Laurice
Leannda
Leanne
Leesa
Lenore
Leonie
Leora
Lesley
Lettitia

Lexa
Lexia
Lexine
Lidiya
Lillian
Lissa
Lita
Lolita
Lona
Lonee
Lonia
Loran
Loreen
Lorene
Lorna
Lurleen
Lurlene
Lydia
Lyn
Lyrie

—M—

Mabel
Maggie
Mais
Majesta
Mallory
Mara
Marcelle
Maree
Margery
Maria
Marietta
Maris
Marji
Marne
Marnie
Marris
Marsha
Marylou
Matilda
Melba
Melissa

Melita
Merna
Merran
Millie
Miranda
Morgana
Morgania

—N—

Nari
Neda
Nellwyn
Nerida
Nerrida
Netta
Neva
Nia
Ninette
Nola
Novelia
Nyssa

—O—

Odette
Oralie
Orlenda
Orlene

—P—

Paisley
Pamella
Paula
Pauline
Peggy
Perl
Peta
Petra
Phenice
Philina
Phoebe
Pollie

Prisilla
Prue

—Q—

Queeny
Quintina

—R—

Rae
Raeleen
Raelene
Raie
Rani
Rea
Rebeka
Reine
Rene
Rhonda
Rihana
Rina

Rochelle
Rosemary

—S—

Sally
Salvina
Selene
Shae
Shan
Shani
Shantelle
Sharni
Shea
Shera
Sherren
Sheryl
Shirley
Shivara
Sibella
Skye
Stella

Suzanna

—T—

Tabia
Tahlia
Topaz
Tricia
Trixy

—U—

Uta

—V—

Valora
Vara
Velika
Verene
Verina
Verna

Veronica
Viki
Virgilia
Viviana
Vivianne

—W—

Wendie
Wilone
Winni

—Y—

Yonina

—Z—

Zenna
Zora
Zorine

Vibration Number 7 Names

—A—

Adelita
Adena
Adore
Adriane
Adrienne
Airley
Alanna
Aleana
Alethea
Alexa
Alexine
Alexis
Alison
Alissa
Alita
Alleece

Alyda
Amanda
Amara
Amberlee
Ambha
Amelita
Ana
Andrea
Anetta
Angelica
Ania
Anne
Annelise
Annette
Annie
Antonina
Arna
Ashley

Ashlyn
Athalia
Avon
Azelle

—B—

Barbara
Beanka
Beatrix
Bessy
Bette
Bliss
Bobina
Bonny
Brie
Brier
Britta

—C—

Cacelia
Cal
Calesta
Camile
Caresse
Carlota
Carissa
Carita
Carli
Carolyn
Catalina
Catharine
Catherina
Caye
Charla
Charline

Cher
Cheri
Chloe
Chrystal
Ciannon
Claresta
Clair
Colline
Corilla
Cyrene

—D—

Danae
Danise
Daron
Deana
Deanne
Delicia
Delcine
Della
Demona
Derora
Desley
Dianna
Diona
Dionetta
Dionne
Dolores
Doreen
Dorene
Dorian

—E—

Ebony
Edana
Edmona
Eleanor
Elizabeth
Ellie
Elyshia
Emelyne
Emlynne

Erinna
Ethyl
Etty
Evania

—F—

Farrah
Faunia
Fern
Flora
Floria
Florinda
Florine
Floris
Francine
Freda
Freida

—G—

Gael
Georgi
Gerlinda
Gladis
Glenda
Goldie
Grace
Guinevere
Gwynne

—H—

Harriet
Hazel
Hedya
Hellene
Hilda
Hollie

—I—

Idona
Indiana

Ingrid

—J—

Jacki
Jacqueline
Jae
Jaimee
Jan
Janela
Jemina
Jenda
Jenni
Jeryl
Jessamyn
Jeynelle
Jill
Jo
Jodie
Joelen
Juli

—K—

Kaele
Kala
Kalinda
Kaila
Kailee
Karla
Karlee
Karolynne
Kasey
Kathryn
Kayse
Keah
Keelia
Kelcey
Kelley
Kerri
Kezia
Kirralee
Kirstienne
Klara

Krystyna

—L—

Larissa
Leathea
Leelah
Lenita
Lila
Lilly
Lizette
Lorelle
Lucy
Lynne

—M—

Madalyn
Magenta
Marcellina
Marija
Marion
Marisa
Marja
Maritza
Marrille
Marrisa
Martha
Maxie
Meg
Melany
Merrielle
Michaela
Mikaela
Millicent
Mirella
Moina
Mona
Monia
Moreen
Morna

—N—

Nadina
Nairee
Nanette
Naomi
Nara
Nathalie
Neera
Nell
Niki
Norma
Nourell
Nova
Novia
Nurice

—O—

Odelet
Odera
Oliana
Ondine
Othelia
Ouriana

—P—

Patrina
Pearl

Penelope
Phedra
Philana
Phyl
Poppy

—Q—

Quintilla

—R—

Raanah
Rachele
Raina
Rana
Rania
Reann
Rebeca
Renae
Renyce
Rheta
Riarna
Rimona
Roberta
Rodina
Romina
Ronda
Ros
Rosalie

Rosalinde
Roschelle
Rosett
Rowe

—S—

Sadira
Saidee
Salena
Sarette
Shamaine
Shana
Sharna
Shellie
Shonalee
Sian
Simmone
Sophey
Stefanie
Steffie
Stephanie
Susannah
Sylvia

—T—

Teri
Terri
Thea

Tyana

—U—

Ula
Ursulina

—V—

Vanna
Vesna
Vicky
Victoria

—W—

Wanda
Willette
Winifred
Wyanet

—Y—

Yanita
Yvette

Vibration Number 8 Names

—A—

Abbey
Abbye
Afra
Alexandra
Alicia
Alletta
Allira
Allyson

Amberleigh
Anabel
Andriana
Angele
Angline
Annaleise
Annaliese
Annemarie
Annwen
Anthia

Arana
Ardella
Aretha
Ariana
Aslyn
Astrid
Athene
Audi
Aurelie
Aylene

Azel

—B—

Bea
Beanca
Benedikta
Bernette
Beryl
Beth

Bethlene
Betsy
Bettina
Beverly
Bo
Brae
Brandie
Brea
Brenda
Briely
Brijette
Brylie

—C—

Caetlyn
Cally
Cammie
Caniel
Carla
Carlee
Carlen
Carline
Cassandra
Cassidy
Caterina
Cathryn
Cayley
Celina
Ceri
Chantelle
Charmine
Chelsea
Cherine
Cheryl
Cindie
Clara
Claretta
Clarinda
Clarine
Cleo
Conny
Crystal
Cynara

Cynthia
Cyrilla

—D—

Dagma
Dagmar
Danelle
Danielle
Daralynn
Daveta
Deborah
Dominique
Doralyn
Dorelle
Dory
Dyan

—E—

Eartha
Edel
Edyth
Elayne
Eleanora
Eliza
Ellene
Elsbeth
Elysia
Emilie
Erika
Erryn
Eryn
Ethelyn
Eugenia

—F—

Faith
Farra
Fawn
Felicity
Felita
Filipa

Fleur
Florisa

—G—

Gabrielle
Gai
Galina
Gaynor
Gelena
Georga
Georgia
Georgine
Gerrie
Gertrude
Glenna
Glennis
Gloria

—H—

Haeli
Heidi
Helen
Henrieka
Henrieta
Hestia
Hetti
Honora
Honoria
Hope

—I—

Iantha
Imelda

—J—

Jacquetta
Jacquith
Jahanne
Jana
Janetta

Janeva
Janine
Janis
Jannette
Jasmine
Jeane
Jeanette
Jeanie
Jenna
Jennee
Jess
Jessalin
Jesseca
Johannah
Jonie
Judi
Julia
Juline
Justine
Justinn

—K—

Kaelene
Kandre
Karin
Karlena
Karmen
Kassey
Kavindra
Kea
Keira
Kendra
Keren
Kerinn
Kerree
Keryl
Khristal
Kolina
Kori
Kristyn
Kylie

—L—

Laila
Laura
Lauren
Lauretta
Lauris
Leah
Leilani
Leota
Leslie
Liliane
Livia
Lizzy
Lucretia
Lurena
Lyndall

—M—

Maarit
Magda
Mahlia
Mali
Marge
Margette
Margie
Marianna
Maridel
Marika
Marissa
Marita
Marjorie
Marli
Martine
Maude
Maye
Melitta
Meriel
Milly
Myna
Myrna

—N—

Natalie
Neralyn
Nicoli
Nikola
Nissa
Nita
Noreen
Norene
Norina

—O—

Odelle
Olwyn
Orlantha

—P—

Pamlena
Phaedra
Phylis
Pia
Pierette
Pierrette
Polly

—Q—

Quenie

—R—

Rahel
Ramona
Rashelle
Ray
Rianon
Romana
Romy
Rosa
Rosetta

—S—

Salli
Samara
Samaria
Sammy
Sarene
Sarina
Savannah
Serena
Shanane
Sheilah
Shellan
Sherona
Sherril
Sibylla
Sidonia
Solana
Sondra
Suzette
Suzie
Sybilla

—T—

Tabatha
Tahnee
Taima
Talara
Talees
Talitha
Tamar
Tamarah
Tamra
Tarin
Tavira
Temina
Therese
Tiarni
Tina
Trina

—V—

Val
Valeska
Venita
Verlie
Vernita
Vikki
Virginia
Viv
Volante

—W—

Wendy
Wenonah
Wilmette

—X—

Xaviera
Xenia
Xylia

—Y—

Yevetta

—Z—

Zabrina
Zuzana

Vibration Number 9 Names

—A—

Acacia
Adele
Alda
Aldith
Allisa
Alma
Almee
Almira
Alva
Andrel
Angeliene
Angelina
Angie
Anika
Anissa
Anita
Anitra
Annora
Ariel
Arlette
Arlie
Ashlie
Astin
Audra
Augusta
Aurelea
Aurie
Azela
Azelia

—B—

Bambi
Beatrice
Belle
Benedicta
Bernadine
Bertha
Bess
Bethia

Betty
Blanche
Blythe
Brenna
Briana
Brianne
Briarley
Brielle
Brigitte
Britni

—C—

Calandia
Calandra
Calysta
Candida
Candie
Carin
Caritta
Carlotta
Carma
Carmen
Carrie
Cassey
Caytie
Chariene
Charmaine
Charmion
Chaise
Chantel
Chelce
Cherelyn
Chrissie
Christal
Clarisa
Coby
Coco
Coleen
Colene
Coralie
Cori

—D—

Dacia
Dalia
Daneta
Danice
Dannika
Danya
Darcee
Darline
Darsey
Dayna
Debbie
Debora
Deidre
Denyse
Derby
Derralie
Destina
Dhani
Dinah
Doralynne
Dulce
Dulcie
Dyana
Dyanne

—E—

Ebbony
Edeline
Edwyna
Elberta
Elia
Elisha
Elly
Elvera
Elvina
Emeline
Erica
Erline
Esmay

Esta
Etti

—F—

Fawnia
Felicia
Fernanda
Fiona
Florey
Frona

—G—

Gabriel
Gais
Garnette
Gena
Geneva
Gennie
Germain
Gillie
Gloriane
Gwenda

—H—

Hattie
Haviva
Heda
Hedia
Helena
Hinda
Holly

—I—

Idalia
Idaline
Idette
Ileen
Ilene

Illona
Imogen
Indi
Inez

—J—

Jacenta
Jacquelyn
Jacynth
Jay
Jayde
Jenelle
Jennifer
Jewelle
Jody
Johanna
Jolynn
Jonina
Jordana
Joscelyne
Judith

—K—

Kacey
Kamara
Karina
Karley
Kasmira
Kathie
Kelcie
Kellie
Kerriann
Khalia
Kirbie
Klarika
Klarissa
Kora
Koria
Kreasha
Kristal

—L—

Lahnee
Lani
Laurell
Laurena
Lea
Leith
Lendra
Lenette
Les
Levina
Liesha
Lina
Linnette
Lise
Lisette
Loralie
Lori
Lorri
Louise
Luanna
Luella
Luwana
Lyndel
Lynnet
Lysanne

—M—

Maddie
Madeline
Mairlee
Malerie
Malia
Malinda
Marcia
Mardi
Margo
Marguerite
Marilee
Maritsa
Marla
Maryse

Maura
Maurine
Mechelle
Melicent
Melina
Melodie
Merlene
Merlina
Merridie
Miriam
Morice
Moriel
Moya
Myrilla

—N—

Nadiya
Nadya
Nanelle
Narissa
Natalina
Nelda
Ngaire
Nicoline
Nikki
Nitara

—O—

Odel
Odessa
Olive
Oona

—P—

Patrice
Patsy
Pattina
Pennie
Phebe
Pierina
Priscilla

—Q—

Quenna

—R—

Ranita
Raya
Regan
Regina
Rexana
Reyna
Richelle
Rivalee
Roanna
Rosalynd
Rosena
Ruthie

—S—

Sadye
Sallee
Sandy
Saralyn
Savanna
Selby
Shandel
Shayne
Sheila
Shelly
Shirah
Shirlene
Sibley
Silvia
Sophie
Starre
Sue

—T—

Tamara
Tammy
Tania

Tanith
Teena
Teneyl
Tennia
Terese
Tesa
Tivona
Tracey
Trudi

—U—

Ullah

Ulli
Una
Ursala

—V—

Valeda
Valerie
Vanessa
Vedette
Verity
Vick
Vicki

Vida
Vivien

—W—

Wenona
Wynne

—Y—

Yasmin
Yolanda
Yolane

Ysabelle

—Z—

Zarah
Zeni
Zia
Zianila
Zola

Vibration Number 11 Names

—A—

Addrenia
Ainslee
Alana
Alfreda
Alithea
Allegra
Andree
Andria
Anelina
Ann
Antoinetta
Antonia
April
Ara
Ardeen
Ardene
Ardeth
Artinka
Asha
Audrey
Aurora

—B—

Beata

Bedelia
Bela
Belinda
Berneta
Bernice
Bev
Beverlee
Biancha
Bridget
Bridie
Brigit
Briony

—C—

Caitrin
Calla
Carilla
Carlynne
Carmita
Cate
Catrin
Celestine
Chaney
Christina
Claudina
Corabel

Corena
Coriss
Correna
Cristin

—D—

Daisie
Damaris
Dana
Deandra
Dearne
Denise
Desiree
Devora
Dianne
Dione
Doretta
Doris

—E—

Eadith
Edrena
Edwardine
Edwina
Eirene

Elenore
Elnora
Eloise
Emlynn
Emmalyn
Erina
Estrella
Evelyn
Ewa

—F—

Fabrienne
Farica
Fayina
Faythe
Florrie

—G—

Garnet
Gayelene
Gilly
Gwendolyn
Gypsy

—H—

Heather
Helyna
Holli

—I—

Idelle
Irena
Irisa
Isa
Isabelle

—J—

Jade
Jileena
Joline
Jordi
Josephine
Josselyn

—K—

Kandice
Karlie
Katrina
Kaya
Kaytlin
Keddie
Kerrilee
Kirby
Kiri
Kittie
Kristian

—L—

Leitia
Lellani
Lenora
Leta
Linnelle

Lorena
Lorraine
Lucille
Lurette
Lynette

—M—

Madelyn
Maisie
Marcella
Margaret
Margarite
Margot
Marian
Marilyn
Marina
Marjie
Marlyn
Martez
Melloney
Melody
Merrille
Midge
Mildred
Mileeta
Mindy
Mirelle
Miriana
Missie
Modesty
Moira
Morganna
Moyanna
Mylene

—N—

Nada
Nadine
Nan
Nanelia
Narida
Neisha

Nerine
Neryl
Ninnette
Nizana
Noleen
Nolene

—O—

Oralia
Orlena
Othilia

—P—

Paige
Pauleen
Paulina
Penny
Penrose
Perle
Petrina
Phalen
Phenica
Phenicia
Pollyanna

—R—

Rachel
Rainie
Raquel
Reina
Renee
Rheannin
Rhianna
Rhona
Rikah
Riki
Robyn
Rolanda
Rosalind
Rozene
Rozina

Rubina

—S—

Shaine
Sharai
Sharne
Sheelagh
Shelli
Shereen
Sommer
Steffi
Stephani
Susan

—T—

Taya
Tracie
Trish

—U—

Ursuline

—V—

Valenaine
Valonia
Varina
Verena
Violet

—W—

Winnie
Winola

—Z—

Zanther
Zenija
Zorina

Vibration Number 22 Names

—A—

Adyth
Afina
Alayne
Alecia
Aleyna
Alleen
Allina
Allix
Allyce
Alvie
Alysia
Anastasia
Angela
Annabel
Anthea
Astred
Athena
Audie
Audre

—B—

Belita
Benne
Betica
Blanch
Blyth
Brit

—C—

Calley
Candace
Candi
Cari
Carol
Cira
Coral
Cree

—D—

Dacie
Daile
Daisy
Danella
Delia
Denys
Devi
Dyane
Dyann

—E—

Echo
Elin
Ellean
Ellena

—F—

Faina

—G—

Gene
Gill
Gina
Glady
Glyn
Gwen

—H—

Haila
Hedda

—I—

Ilyssa
Isabeau

—J—

Jacinta
Janina
Jeanne
Jessie
Jewell
Josie
Joyce
Juanita
Judie
Julina
Juniata
Justina

—K—

Karen
Karlana
Karly
Karra
Kathi
Kaylah
Kiara
Kitty
Krysta
Kylee

—L—

Lari
Lealia
Lily
Linda
Luanne

—M—

Manuela
Marjy
Marya
Marys
Megan
Missy
Musette

—N—

Noleta

—O—

Odella

—R—

Raissa
Raye
Roana
Ruth

—S—

Sachi
Sadelle
Sallie
Sarena
Shaye
Sofi
Sonia
Sybil
Sylvana

—T—

Tandra
Teare
Toni
Tracy

—U—

Uria

–V–

Veleda

–W–

Wilma

–Y–

Yani

–Z–

Zaneta

MALE NAMES LIST

Vibration Number 1 Names

—A—

Abbe
Abbie
Adam
Adin
Ainsworth
Alain
Alan
Aldrich
Aleren
Alf
Alfonso
Alfred
Alisdair
Allyn
Ambrose
Anselm
Anton
Antoni
Archy
Ardin
Ari
Arnold
Arve
Arvin
Ashby

—B—

Baillee
Barry
Beaumont
Beecher
Blaze
Bob
Bobby
Boyd
Brant
Brice
Buck
Burgess
Byrne

—C—

Cairns
Call
Campbell
Charlton
Claude
Clifford
Conn
Conrad
Corwin
Crofton
Crosby
Cy

—D—

Damien
Dan
Danby
Dani
Darick
Darrick
Darrin
Davis
Dempster
Dene
Dennett
Des
Desi
Dewie
Dolf
Dolph
Dupre

—E—

Eden
Edmond
Edward
Edwin
Elias
Erick
Erin
Everard
Ezera

—F—

Fadel
Feyne
Fitch

Flinn
Frankie
Fremont

—G—

Garik
Garrik
Gawain
Gerry
Gil
Gilbert
Gilby
Giovanni
Glenister
Gordon
Granville
Greg
Greig

—H—

Hadan
Haddon
Hadley
Hanin
Hanleigh
Harod
Harris
Harrod
Hermann
Hilliard

—I—

Ignatius
Irwin
Ivan
Ivers
Ives
Ivor

—J—

Jackson
Jael
Jed
Jedediah
Jesper
Joey
Josef
Joseph
Juan

—K—

Kayde
Kelby
Kelvin
Kingston
Kirkley
Kleeton
Kyne

—L—

Lancelot
Landers
Leon
Leron
Lewes
Lirone
Locke
Lorand
Lukas
Lynton

—M—

Mack
Martyn
Melvyn
Meredith
Merwin
Meryl
Mikkell

Mitchell
Montgomery

—N—

Neale
Newton
Nially
Nick
Noel
Nyall

—O—

Olly
Orland
Orton
Osbourne
Oxford

—P—

Pablo
Pat
Perry
Peter
Phillip

—Q—

Quentin

—R—

Radcliffe
Rade
Ralph
Ravinder
Raynor
Reagan
Redmond
Reeve
Rein
Rickard

Rickie
Ridley
Robb
Roddie
Ridley
Rogan
Rohin
Roland
Roldan
Ronald

—S—

Sawyer
Sherard
Sherrard
Skip
Sol
Stacey
Sutton
Sylvester

—T—

Taite
Tarquin
Tate
Taylor
Thaddeus
Thorpe
Tilden
Trelawny
Tristram
Tyen

—U—

Uziel

—V—

Vachil
Valerian
Vaughn

Verne
Vian
Vinnie

—*W*—

Waldo

Wally
Ward
Weldon
Wellesley
Wilhelm

—*Z*—

Zane
Zuriel

Vibration Number 2 Names

—*A*—

Abel
Adley
Adrian
Aerin
Aidan
Alasdair
Albie
Aldric
Alek
Aleron
Alleyne
Ancell
Andrew
Arne
Arnie
Aubin
Audric

—*B*—

Bailie
Barney
Bartley
Bentley
Berton
Blain
Boyden
Brett
Buddy
Byron

—*C*—

Callen
Carlton
Carter
Cary
Chandler
Chapman
Charlie
Christian
Collin
Conor
Corbett
Cowan
Craig
Cromwell

—*D*—

Dacey
Dall
Damon
Dana
Dannie
Daryle
Deane
Delwyn
Demetri
Dennis
Deon
Desmond
Dewain

Digby
Donn
Donnelly
Dorren
Doug
Durante
Dylan

—*E*—

Eddy
Elson
Elwood
Emmet
Everley

—*F*—

Felix
Fenton
Forbes
Franklyn
Frazer
Frazier
Fredie

—*G*—

Galvin
Garey
Gerald
Glen

Griffith
Gus
Gustaf

—*H*—

Haines
Hallam
Hamilton
Hanan
Hanley
Hardy
Hart
Henrik
Herbie
Hervey
Hubert
Hyatt

—*I*—

Innis
Isaiah
Izak

—*J*—

Jaime
Jared
Javier
Jerad
Jere

Jereme
Jervis
John
Jonathan
Joshua
Judson
Julius

—K—

Kale
Kanil
Kavanagh
Kayne
Kearny
Kegan
Kelly
Kendal
Kev
Kirby
Kristian
Kynan

—L—

Lache
Larry
Lathan
Leobold
Lucais
Lynn

—M—

Machial
Mardon
Marian
Markus
Marx

Max
Mike
Milton
Morris
Myles

—N—

Nevan
Nevins
Nigel
Nilson
Noah
Nolan
Normie
Norvin
Norward

—O—

Omar
Orrin
Orville
Oscar
Oswald

—P—

Page
Paige
Phelan
Pierce
Porter
Powell
Pryor

—Q—

Quinton

—R—

Radley
Rainer
Reuben
Rex
Rik
Riki
Roderick
Rohan
Rolfe
Rolphe
Ron
Rydder
Ryland

—S—

Sandi
Saunders
Savin
Seaton
Shane
Shawn
Sheffield
Sullivan
Sydney

—T—

Tarrant
Ted
Teddie
Timothy
Tomlin
Tony
Torey
Torrey
Trace

Travus
Tremayne
Tristan
Tynan

—U—

Ulrick
Uriel

—V—

Varian
Vaughan

—W—

Wain
Wallache
Walt
Warrick
Watson
Webster
Werner
Wes
Wiley
Will

—X—

Xever

—Z—

Zeke

Vibration Number 3 Names

—*A*—

Abby
Addison
Airell
Alban
Alec
Aleks
Alexander
Algar
Alister
Allard
Arch
Arnan
Aron
Arron
Art
Austin
Awan
Azur

—*B*—

Bales
Barthel
Bastian
Beauen
Ben
Bern
Bevis
Blaise
Bradden
Branton
Bren
Brien
Brod
Bryson
Burke

—*C*—

Cale
Carlin
Carney
Charles
Cheston
Chris
Clarance
Colbert
Colby
Corey
Cornall
Coryden
Cyrille

—*D*—

Dalton
Darnell
Davey
Declan
Del
Delmer
Demetris
Dermot
Derryn
Devlin
Dillon
Doane
Drake
Drydan
Duncan
Dunstan

—*E*—

Eamon
Edison
Eldred
Elliott
Ellis
Elroy
Elsworth
Elton
Emery
Emil
Emmanuel
Ethan

—*F*—

Fairleigh
Farleigh
Ferdinand
Ferris
Findley
Florian
Franky

—*G*—

Galvan
Garcia
George
Georgie
Glennard
Graham
Grantley

—*H*—

Hal
Halbert
Hamel
Hamlin
Hanford
Harrison
Hayden
Howell

—*J*—

James
Janie
Jarrod
Jayson
Jeffrey
Jereth
Jerome
Jerrome
Jevon
Joe
Johan
Johnnie
Jon
Jonah
Judd
Justin

—*K*—

Kade
Kaela
Keaton
Ken
Kerrin
Keven
Kingsley
Kiryl
Kris

—*L*—

Ladd
Laurie
Lawson
Leland
Leonardo
Leroy
Lindsay
Linton
Lou
Luther
Lyell
Lyndon
Lyon
Lyron

—M—

Madison
Manuel
Marcus
Marshall
Martie
Martin
Mathian
Mel
Melvin
Mickey
Moore
Morrell
Mortimer

—N—

Nathaniel
Neron
Newlyn
Nickolas
Norman
Norris

—O—

Odell

Olery
Oran
Orian
Otway
Owen

—P—

Pascale
Pearce
Prentiss

—Q—

Quinn

—R—

Rawley
Reg
Ricky
Roddy
Royce
Ryhan

—S—

Scot

Seaden
Sean
Shelton
Silvester
Simeon
Steele
Syd

—T—

Thaine
Thane
Theo
Tobias
Tom
Tyson

—U—

Uriah

—V—

Vallis
Vinny
Vinson
Vlad
Volney

—W—

Wallace
Willis
Wilton

—X—

Xends

—Z—

Zachariah

Vibration Number 4 Names

—A—

Abbot
Adriel
Ainsley
Al
Alayne
Albert
Alby
Aldrick
Allan
Alvin

Amiel
Archibald
Arny
Avel

—B—

Barnie
Benji
Billie
Blake
Borden

Bradley
Braeden
Braith
Brendan
Brion
Broden
Broderick
Bruce
Budd

—C—

Christopher
Cleon
Clyde
Corydon
Cullen
Cyril

—D—

Dael
Dale
Dallas
Danny
Darrel
David
Delmor
Delwin
Demitry
Deniz
Denney
Dennison
Denys
Dev
Dexter
Dilan
Dominic
Donall
Donnell
Donovan

—E—

Elvis
Emory
Etan

—F—

Fairley
Falkner
Farley
Felice
Fergus
Finlay
Franklin
Fraser
Fredy
Frederich
Frederik

—G—

Garrard
Garrick
Gill
Glyn
Graeme

—H—

Harold
Haydon
Herbert
Herby
Herve
Howey
Huntlee
Hylton

—J—

Jarryd
Jeremy
Jermyn
Jerry
Jesse
Jethro
Jose
Jotham
Jude
Jules
Juri
Jye

—K—

Kane
Kavan
Kean
Keene
Kennard
Kennie
Kieran
Kit

Kristofer
Kym

—L—

Lee
Len
Lionel
Louis
Lucus
Luke

—M—

Martain
Maynard
Melburn
Miles
Milo
Monte
Morrison
Myron

—N—

Nataniel
Nathanael
Neil
Nevile
Normy

—O—

Orford

—P—

Patric
Percy
Perren

—R—

Reynard

Reyne
Robin
Rory
Roy
Ruari
Rudolf
Rudolph

—S—

Sebastien
Shannon
Shelden
Sherwyn
Sidney
Sinclair
Solomon
Steven

—T—

Taman
Tane
Tara
Tawrin
Teddy
Terrill
Theobald
Thomas
Timeon

—V—

Vale
Vaun
Vyron

—W—

Wallis
Wilbur
Wilfred
Wright

Vibration Number 5 Names

—A—

Adir
Alair
Aland
Aldan
Alein
Aleck
Alen
Algernon
Alvan
Argyle
Arlen
Arthur
Ashland
Ashlen
Ashton
Auburn
Aydon

—B—

Baillie
Ballard
Barnes
Baron
Barron
Bart
Benjamin
Bertie
Bertram
Bowen
Boyce
Bradford
Bramwell
Brandon
Brandt
Brent
Bryn

—C—

Cable
Caleb
Carlos
Cecil
Clarke
Clay
Clemente
Colvert
Con
Cyrus

—D—

Dai
Darby
Dave
Davie
Davin
Delsen
Den
Denby
Derick
Derrick
Dew
Dermott
Dom
Donahue
Donald
Drew
Duke

—E—

Earle
Ellery
Ellison
Ellwood
Errol
Everett
Evin

Ezra

—F—

Faber
Fernando
Fletcher
Francklyn
Frank
Frederic

—G—

Gardell
Gareth
Garmon
Garran
Garreth
Gascon
Gawen
Georgy
Gervase
Gilmour
Gilroy
Gregory
Gustave
Gusten

—H—

Haddan
Haden
Haiden
Hamlet
Hammond
Hansel
Harlow
Hedley
Henleigh
Herman
Herod
Herrod

Homer
Horace

—I—

Isaak
Ivar

—J—

Jal
Jason
Jayden
Jaye
Jedd
Jim
Jimmie
Joachim
Johnny

—K—

Kass
Kayd
Keenan
Kendall
Kenneth
Kent
Kilby
Kinsley
Kiril
Krist

—L—

Laidley
Laine
Lane
Leif
Leigh
Leo
Lennie

Lewien
Lewis
Lindell
Lindon
Linley
Liron
Lloyd
Lorrie
Lowrence

—*M*—

Madden
Mallery
Marty
Marvin
Mathieu
Merrick
Michel
Mickie
Mikel
Morgan
Morton

—*N*—

Ned
Nev
Newlin
Niels

Niles
Norwood

—*O*—

Ordway
Osbourn
Ovid

—*P*—

Paddy
Patton
Paul
Penley
Percival
Peyton

—*Q*—

Quillan
Quintin

—*R*—

Raymon
Rede
Reed
Rick
Ricki

Riddley
Rodd
Ronny

—*S*—

Sanford
Scott
Sedgley
Selden
Serle
Sheldon
Sherborne
Sid
Slade
Stacy
Stanleigh
Sterling
Sutherland
Symon

—*T*—

Tait
Tannar
Tasman
Terone
Terry
Thornton
Trent

—*U*—

Udall
Upton
Urias

—*V*—

Verden
Vere
Vern

—*W*—

Walden
Wayne
Webb
Whitney

—*X*—

Xenos

—*Z*—

Zacharias
Zack
Zainol

Vibration Number 6 Names

—*A*—

Abbner
Abbott
Abey
Adair
Adar
Adner
Adrien
Alcot

Aldridge
Alfie
Alleyn
Allister
Alrik
Alvy
Andre
Ansel
Aram
Arden

Arie
Arni
Asher
Aston

—*B*—

Bartholomew
Bayden
Benny

Billy
Blair
Bobie
Boone
Brayden
Bretlyn
Bryan
Brydon

—C—

Cameron
Cedric
Chester
Cheyne
Clem
Clinton
Clive
Cordell
Coridon
Crandell
Crompton

—D—

Damian
Dane
Daren
Darren
Darryl
Daryl
Dean
Demetrius
Dempsey
Denis
Dex
Dion
Dirk
Don
Druce
Durant
Dustin

—E—

Edan
Eman
Emlyn
Ernie
Erwin
Evan
Evers

—F—

Fabian
Farant
Farlie
Frayne
Fred
Freddie
Fyfe

—G—

Garek
Garret
Garry
Garvey
Gary
Ginson
Grant
Griffin
Guston
Gwyn

—H—

Hailey
Haley
Heath
Hector
Hendrik
Henley
Herb
Hilton
Howard
Howe
Howie
Humbert
Humphrey
Huntley
Hurd
Hurlee

—I—

Iain
Ian
Isaac
Ivon

—J—

Jasper
Jeremiah
Jevin
Joel

—K—

Karl
Karson
Keelby
Kele
Kennet
Kenny
Kerel
Kiral
Kory

—L—

Lachlan
Layton
Leonard
Lerone
Lesley
Lyn

—M—

Malcolm
Mallory
Mayson
Michael
Mikael
Millard
Morven

Murray

—N—

Noland
Norm
Norton

—O—

Oakes
Oakley
Orlan

—P—

Parnell
Patrick
Perryn
Pierson

—R—

Radburn
Raleigh
Raymund
Reade
Reggie
Renn
Rian
Riklee
Riley
Robbie
Robert
Rolf
Rowland
Ryle

—S—

Sam
Sammie
Seamus
Selvon

Shan
Shaughn
Sheehan
Sheridan
Simen
Spenser
Stanley
Stephen

—T—

Talbert
Taryn

Tedd
Tildan
Tim
Torry
Tory
Troy
Turner
Tymon
Tyran

—V—

Vachel

Vane
Varner
Victor
Vincent

—W—

Wacian
Wade
Waldon
Whitby
Winston
Wren

—Z—

Zeb
Zedekiah

Vibration Number 7 Names

—A—

Adon
Aivars
Alben
Alger
Allayne
Alric
Alson
Alten
Anders
Anthony
Ardean
Ardon
Arley
Armon

—B—

Bailee
Baird
Basil
Baxter
Bede
Beldon
Berty
Brad

Bram
Brenton
Bronson
Burt

—C—

Cal
Calder
Callan
Calvin
Carey
Carl
Chad
Clarence
Clee
Clifton
Colton
Corbin
Cornell
Crawford
Crispin
Curtice
Cyrill

—D—

Daron
Darrell
Derek
Dewit
Dieter
Dietrick
Dinos
Dinsmore
Donnie
Doran
Dorian
Dorran
Douglas
Doyle
Dryden
Dyami
Dyre

—E—

Eardley
Edmund
Eldrid
Ellard
Erelyn

Erich
Erik
Ewan

—F—

Faulkner
Finn
Francis
Francklin
Frederick
Fritz

—G—

Galven
Garald
Giles
Gilmore
Ginton
Glenden
Glenn
Granger
Grantley
Guthrie

—H—

Hamil
Hamnet
Hank
Harry
Hartleigh
Harvey
Henry

—I—

Indiana
Innes
Irving

—J—

Jack
Jae
Jamari
Jan
Jarad
Jarrin
Jarvis
Jenda
Jeth
Jevan
Jimmy
Jonathon
Jori
Josh

—K—

Kalleb
Karsten
Keegan
Keir
Kelley
Kenton

Ker
Kerem
Kerr
Kevin
Kingsly
Kipp
Kurt

—L—

Laurence
Lawry
Lenny
Lester
Lindsey
Lorry
Lowell

—M—

Maccallum
Mark
Mathew
Maurice
Mervyn
Mic
Mikkel
Muir

—N—

Navarre
Neill
Nelson
Neville
Niki
Norrie

—O—

Oren

Ormond
Orren
Osborne

—P—

Pascal
Payne
Paxon

—Q—

Quennel
Quin
Quinby
Quinlan

—R—

Randolph
Ramon
Reginald
Remington
Rhys
Richard
Richie
Rigby
Rikleigh
Riordan
Rodian
Ronn
Russell
Ryder
Rylan

—S—

Seth
Simon
Stanford
Stewart

—T—

Talbot
Tavish
Terence
Terrence
Thorby
Todd
Trenton
Tyrone

—U—

Udale
Uland
Ulwin

—V—

Valente
Valle
Vic
Vladimir
Volny

—W—

Walter
Warner
Warren
Warwick
William
Willie

—X—

Xavier

Vibration Number 8 Names

—A—

Abbey
Abe
Abie
Abraham
Aimrey
Alaric
Albion
Alcott
Aldred
Allen
Alroy
Alton
Amery
Andy
Antony
Archie
Arkin
Arnon
Arte
Artie
Athan
Austen
Avery
Aziel

—B—

Baden
Barclay
Barlow
Barnett
Barrie
Benedict
Benn
Bernard
Bernie
Berwin
Bevan
Bill
Braden

Brenden
Brian
Brodie
Bryce
Bryant

—C—

Cadby
Callum
Cam
Casey
Chadwick
Chene
Clemens
Cole
Colin
Constantine
Cornelius
Curt

—D—

Dal
Darnall
Dayn
Delmar
Denny
Denten
Desmund
Devlen
Dewey
Drydon
Durand
Durward
Durwin
Dwight

—E—

Eamonn
Edgar

Eldin
Emanuel
Emerson
Emile
Eric

—F—

Fane
Farand
Farly
Farrand
Favian
Felten
Findlay
Finley
Floyd
Flynn

—G—

Gallagher
Garrett
Garvin
Gavin
Gerard
Giuseppe
Glendon
Godfrey
Gregg
Guy

—H—

Hadlee
Halden
Hale
Hamlen
Harel
Harlin
Hartley
Hoghan

Hugh
Hurley

—I—

Inness

—J—

Javas
Jeames
Jedidiak
Jess
Jordan
Joshia
Judah
Justis
Jy

—K—

Keith
Kelvyn
Kenleigh
Kenn
Kennett
Kera
Kerwin
Kevan
Kurtis
Kyle

—L—

Lance
Laughton
Leslie
Liam
Louie

—M—

Mac
Maison
Mal
Marc
Marten
Mason
Milburn

—N—

Neall
Nealson
Nevil
Newlynn
Nye
Nyjal

—O—

Ollie
Orion
Osburn
Osmond

—P—

Perrin
Prescott
Preston

—Q—

Quincy

—R—

Radbourne
Raimund
Randall
Ranon
Ray
Reamonn
Rhett
Ridgley
Rob
Ronan
Ross
Roulston
Rowan

Rowley
Royd
Rupert

—S—

Sammy
Samuel
Sanders
Saul
Seath
Seedon
Selwyn
Shannan
Shelby
Simson
Skipp
Spencer
Stafford
Steve
Stevie

—T—

Tavis

Theron
Timon
Toby
Torrence
Travis
Tremain
Trevor
Treyvaud
Tyler

—V—

Vail
Valerius
Vince

—W—

Wallie
Waylen
Wells
Wesley

Vibration Number 9 Names

—A—

Adal
Adlar
Alard
Alastair
Alden
Aleksander
Alrick
Alston
Alvis
Amory
Ansell
Anson
Arel

Arlie
Arlin
Arvid
Ashlin
Aubrey
Audwin

—B—

Bailey
Benjie
Bert
Brendon
Bret
Bromley

Bud
Buddie
Burton
Butch

—C—

Cain
Calvert
Charley
Chase
Ches
Chilton
Clayton
Clement

Cliff
Coleman
Conal
Conroy
Conway
Corbet
Corby
Creighton
Crichton
Culbert
Curtis

—D—

Dagan

Daniel
Darius
Darton
Delsin
Denton
Devin
Dewitt
Dick
Donny
Duane
Dwayne

—E—

Earl
Ed
Eddie
Egan
Eliott
Elwin
Ernest

—F—

Felten
Fidel

—G—

Gabel
Gable
Gabriel
Garner
Garth
Geordie
Gervais
Glynn
Grayson
Gustav
Gustin

—H—

Hadden

Hadleigh
Hared
Harlan
Hendrick
Henri
Henryk
Hew
Hewett
Hogan
Holmes

—J—

Jahya
Jake
Jamey
Jamil
Jay
Jayme
Jaymin
Jeff

—K—

Kallem
Keane
Kendell
Kenley
Kess
Kienan
Kiernan
Kingsten
Konrad

—L—

Lawrence
Leighton
Leith
Llewelyn
Lyle

—M—

Manning
Marius
Marshal
Matt
Matthew
Matthiew
Maximillian
Maxwell
Meldon
Melville
Mick

—N—

Nial
Nicholas
Nikki
Norry
Nowell

—O—

Oliver
Olivier
Orson
Otman

—P—

Paine
Paxton
Phil
Prentice

—R—

Radborn
Rainger
Ralston
Ramsey
Randel
Rawson

Rayburn
Raymond
Rayne
Reece
Reid
Ridleigh
Ritchie
Rodney
Roger
Rollins
Royden

—S—

Sandy
Sebastian
Selby
Shayne
Sherborn
Stan
Stanfield
Stirling
Strahan
Stuart
Syman

—T—

Tanis
Teddey
Theodore
Tiernan
Tolemy
Ty

—U—

Udell
Ulric
Urian
Uzziel

—V—	—W—	Willy	—Z—
Vachell	Wal	Woodley	Zared
Vance	Walby		Zelik
Vasil	Walsh	—X—	
Vick	Waring		
Vin	Waylon	Xeros	
		Xylon	

Vibration Number 11 Names

—A—	Dannie	Hubert	—N—
Abel	Demetri		Nigel
Adrian	Dennis	—I—	Normie
Aldric	Desmond		
Alek	Donnelly	Isaiah	—R—
Andrew	Dorren		
Arnie	Durante	—J—	Rolfe
Audric			Rolphe
	—E—	Jai	
—B—		Jonathan	—T—
	Evelyn	Justus	
Barney			Teddie
	—F—	—K—	Timothy
—C—			
	Felix	Kale	—W—
Chandler	Forbes	Kev	
Chapman	Fredie	Kristian	Walt
Charlie			Wes
Christian	—G—	—L—	
Collin			—Z—
Corbett	Garey	Larry	
Craig	Gerald	Lucas	Zak
Cromwell	Gus		
		—M—	
—D—	—H—		
		Max	
Dall	Herbie	Milton	
	Hervey		

Vibration Number 22 Names

—A—

Aaron
Albert
Alder
Aldin
Alvin
Amiel
Arny
Arvel
Ayden

—B—

Baily
Barth
Benji
Bracy
Brock
Bruce

—C—

Camden
Chane
Cleon
Cullen

—D—

Dalston
Danny
David
Dayne
Denys
Dilan
Donall
Dreau

—E—

Elden
Elston
Elvis
Emmett

—G—

Gene
Gill
Glyn

—H—

Haldan

—J—

Jaron
Jotham
Julian
Juri

—K—

Kaine
Keene
Kelbee
Kellby
Kirk

—L—

Lawton
Logan
Louis

—M—

Malcon
Meldan
Miles
Milo
Monte

—N—

Nathan
Neil

—P—

Penn

—R—

Roy
Ryan

—S—

Seadon
Stanton
Steven
Symen

—T—

Teddy
Thomas
Twain
Tysson

—V—

Valdis

—W—

Waite
Walton